WHAT COMES NEXT

WHAT COMES NEXT

40 DAYS OF HEALING AFTER HEARTBREAK, BURNOUT, OR BROKENNESS

JESS CONNOLLY

a division of Baker Publishing Group
Grand Rapids, Michigan

Published by Baker Books
a division of Baker Publishing Group
Grand Rapids, Michigan
BakerBooks.com

Printed in China

Library of Congress Cataloging-in-Publication Data
Names: Connolly, Jess, author.
Title: What comes next : 40 days of healing after heartbreak, burnout, or brokenness / Jess Connolly.
Description: Grand Rapids, Michigan : Baker Books, a division of Baker Publishing Group, 2025.
Identifiers: LCCN 2024059528 | ISBN 9781540902559 (cloth) | ISBN 9781493451081 (ebook)
Subjects: LCSH: Healing—Religious aspects—Christianity—Prayers and devotions. | Suffering—Religious aspects—Christianity—Prayers and devotions. | Christian women—Religious life. | Devotional exercises.
Classification: LCC BT732 .C67 2025 | DDC 242/.4—dc23/eng/20250215
LC record available at https://lccn.loc.gov/2024059528

Cover design by Riley Moody

The author is represented by Illuminate Literary Agency www.illuminateliterary.com

Baker Publishing Group publications use paper produced from sustainable forestry practices and postconsumer waste whenever possible.

25 26 27 28 29 30 31 7 6 5 4 3 2 1

In honor of Poppy
and the apostle Paul.

DAY 1

This Is Where It Gets Good

My grace is all you need. My power works best in weakness.

2 Corinthians 12:9 NLT

The moments when your knees hit the floor.

When your stomach drops.

When the doctor says the thing, and all of a sudden, you can't breathe.

When the door closes behind the person you never thought would leave.

Or maybe nothing happens, but you look around and think, *How in the world did we get here? How did things get so upside down?*

What comes next?

This book is for the people on the other side of those heart-wrenching seconds. Whether it's been two days or twenty years, this book is for those trying to stand back up, keep food down, take deep breaths, trust again, breathe again, live again, and wake up their soul. This is for the ones who have a sliver of hope that maybe—just maybe—there is life after our breaking points of pain, fatigue, and failure.

I will be the first to tell you that my faith sometimes falters in moments of crisis and in seasons of great pain. I used to feel ashamed about that, but now I know that it actually takes great faith to whisper to God in the dark, "Are You sure You're real?"

It actually takes great faith to whisper—or scream—"What's next?"

The problem is that we have so much to lose when we let that whisper linger and become our new narrative. Even more than what we've already lost: people, time, hope, or blessing. And here's why: When the whisper becomes the song of our season, we stop believing that God is good and that God is real. And if God is not real—if Jesus didn't die for our sins and rise with our redemption in hand, if the Holy Spirit who hovered over the waters at creation is not alive and active in our lives—we have everything to lose. Many of us have staked our whole lives, families, vocations, rhythms, communities, and worldviews on trusting that God is real and that He is good.

I no longer shame myself when moments of pain cause me to doubt His existence or His trustworthiness. I don't believe He is dismayed by my humanity or the finite limits of my faith. But I also try not to let those moments become seasons. Instead, I double down on trying to believe this truth: that what comes next, the breakthroughs, are what make the breakdowns in faith worth it.

What comes next, the healing, meets us in our heartbreak.

What comes next, the renewal, is what makes the heart-wrenching moments of doubt seem fleeting.

What comes next is where it gets good.

Maybe not circumstantially—maybe nothing on the surface changes—but when the women of God dig down deep and ask for healing in the midst of heartache, the spiritual atmosphere shifts.

Together, on this first day of healing, let's read some of the apostle Paul's words about a hardship in his life:

> If I wanted to boast, I would be no fool in doing so, because I would be telling the truth. But I won't do it, because I don't want anyone to give me credit beyond what they can see in my life or hear in my message, even though I have received such wonderful revelations from God. So to keep me from becoming proud, I was given a thorn in my flesh, a messenger from Satan to torment me and keep me from becoming proud.
>
> Three different times I begged the Lord to take it away. Each time he said, "My grace is all you need. My power works best in weakness." So now I am glad to boast about my weaknesses, so that the power of Christ can work through me. That's why I take pleasure in my weaknesses, and in the insults, hardships, persecutions, and troubles that I suffer for Christ. For when I am weak, then I am strong. (2 Cor. 12:6–10 NLT)

Paul is writing to a church that he established, and he keeps visiting them and sending them letters warning them that they are being led astray. The Judaizers were essentially preaching a false gospel, and Paul was zealous for the church to remember that weakness and pain do not negate God's power in our lives. Moreover, weakness and pain are often the exact setting God uses to do what only He can do.

To communicate this, Paul uses his own pain. He points to a malady that he has been unable to get rid of to show the Corinthians, *Look, I am just like you. I can live for God and still experience hardship. I can obey God, and it might still look like I'm losing. I can show up exhausted and defeated, and even have others wonder what in the world is wrong with me, but I'm right where God wants me to be.*

Because *this* is the gospel: Christ died for us, not because we were tidy, great, and full of potential. Instead, God sent His own Son at just the right time because He was motivated by love for us. And by the power of the Holy Spirit, Christ rose from the grave with our redemption in hand, not so that we could experience easy, perfect lives but so that we could experience redemption here on earth and ultimately in heaven.

And so, here is the good news for you and me today: When the reality of our very real, very good God breaks through in our weakest moments—this is where it gets good.

What's next for us is God's power made perfect in our weakness so that He might be glorified and we might be reconciled to Him and to one another.

I can't promise that your heartbreak, burnout, and brokenness will immediately dissipate. But I will stake my whole life on this principle: The weaker we are, the louder we will cry out and cling to God.

For these first ten days, we will let God care for us in the middle of our weakness. Today, we're going to begin by mustering up all the faith, hope, and desperation we've got to declare over our lives, *This is where it gets good.* We don't know what's next in the physical world, but we know what's next spiritually: God's power made perfect.

Spend a few minutes reflecting on the following questions. Then read today's affirmation, praying for a breakthrough.

REFLECTION QUESTIONS

1. On a scale of 1–10, how scared are you to trust God with your current weakness?
2. Take a moment to consider what options you have, opposite of acknowledging your weaknesses. What else could you do? Hide? Pretend? Puff up with pride?
3. What keeps you from saying about your weakness, "This is where it gets good"?
4. Can you speak the following affirmation over yourself, even if no one else joins you?

TODAY'S AFFIRMATION

I am a child of God, and I boast in the gospel of grace. This means that I don't boast in my success, blessings, or worldly accolades that others might praise me for. I may be experiencing heartbreak, burnout, and brokenness in my life, but I believe that God is real and that God is good. The banner over my life is redemption, the calling on my life is intact, and the power of God in my life is not negated by any circumstances—in Jesus's name. This is where it gets good because God is here, and His power is made perfect in weakness.

DAY 2

Don’t Grow Cold

When I kept it all inside,
  my bones turned to powder,
  my words became daylong groans.

The pressure never let up;
  all the juices of my life dried up.

Psalm 32:3–4 MSG

She kept asking about my temperature.

“Are you feeling warm?”

“Are you cold?”

I was in a counseling session with my long-trusted therapist. Some might call it an emergency therapy session. I’d emailed her a desperate message after something incredibly surprising, traumatic, and sad had happened in my immediate family. She made space in her schedule, I showed up, disheveled, with a tearstained face, and we got to work.

But as we talked, she kept asking about my temperature, and I found it a little odd.

At the end of the session, she explained why: Often, when people are dissociating or when they're experiencing trauma or shock, their bodies feel cold. You might even feel physically cold if you're emotionally freezing, living in fight-or-flight. She didn't want to end the session until I felt warm.

As soon as she explained this, I thought about two different traumatic events I had experienced in the last year: one where I felt emotionally and physically cold and almost removed from what was happening, and the other where my body groaned with grief and my physical and emotional temperature rose to a boiling point. I didn't feel shame about the way I experienced one versus the other, but I did note that the event that left my face hot with tears and my body toasty with visceral waves of pain left me far closer to healing than the other.

This is one of those little facts that makes me marvel at God. He allows our bodies to live and breathe through the most horrific things. He empowers us to keep going when it seems incredibly reasonable to just give up.

For you, just opening this book was a step toward warming up, even if you feel you've grown cold from pain or fatigue. Turning the page to today's entry might be the most courageous and hopeful thing you have done after a prolonged season of numbness and cold.

And this temptation to turn off our feelings—to shut down, freeze, push through without passion, stuff down our emotions, and act like everything is fine and nothing is difficult—we come by it honestly. We were born into a culture that praises women for pretending to be strong and stoic. We compliment those who can make it through a funeral without crying. We bless composure and favor the detached, mistaking a frozen soul for strength instead of seeing it as a coping mechanism that deserves compassion.

And this is why I'm so thankful for the Psalms. For all his faults, David—the guy God referred to as a man after His own heart—was incredible at "staying warm." He didn't pretend that he didn't need God. He didn't see emotions, loss, or longing as a threat to his intimacy with the Father but rather as a conduit to connecting with his one true King.

And I love Psalm 32 in particular, where David paints a picture of what happens when we live "cold" for too long:

> When I refused to confess my sin,
> my body wasted away,
> and I groaned all day long.
> Day and night your hand of discipline was heavy on me.
> My strength evaporated like water in the summer heat.
>
> Finally, I confessed all my sins to you
> and stopped trying to hide my guilt.
> I said to myself, "I will confess my rebellion to the Lord."
> And you forgave me! All my guilt is gone.
> (Ps. 32:3–5 NLT)

One of David's most well-known weaknesses (read: sins) was demonstrated when he abused his power and took Bathsheba, the wife of his soldier Uriah, for himself. Then, to hide his sin when Bathsheba became pregnant, David sent Uriah to the front lines of war to die. In the wake of his sin and the ripple effect of pain that it caused in the lives of so many, David wrote Psalm 51, a beautiful hymn of repentance. After he confessed his sins, he wrote Psalm 32. Knowing the order of when these psalms were written, it strikes me that David was warming up to the knowledge of his own weakness.

For most of us, the pain we are currently in probably isn't because we have sinned to the same degree or manner as David.

We are most likely experiencing heartbreak, burnout, and brokenness due to a smattering of things happening around us, or even to us. Even still, I believe we can find wild encouragement in David's words, and even some warning against what happens if we dissociate from our emotions, our needs, or even our thoughts for too long.

I don't know about you, but I have often sensed that my "bones might turn to powder," so I know exactly what Eugene Peterson (the author of *The Message* paraphrase of the Bible) means when he describes a "daylong groan."

Shame off you if you've been coping by letting your heart, your mind, your soul, your longings, and even your grief stay cold. Shame off you if you've let little parts of yourself grow cold to protect you from the pain, pressure, fatigue, or fear of what comes next.

But there is another way. The way we heal, the path to waking up and navigating into a new story—the one God has written for us—is making sure we're warm. And the way we get warm is by talking to God about how we got here and how it feels now that we find ourselves in this space. Simply put, we can't ask, "What's next?" until we ask, "What is happening now, and how do I feel about it?"

It may take courage, it will take trusting God, but I believe that a month from now, a year from now, even a decade from now, we will be grateful that we chose to stay warm instead of letting our hearts grow cold.

REFLECTION QUESTIONS

1. Do you feel warm or cold right now? Is it physical, emotional, or both?
2. Take a moment to note how you've been praised or corrected for your emotional response to pain in the past. Do you think God would agree with what's been spoken over you?
3. What are the thoughts, fears, and problems that you'd rather not address right now? Can you share them with God, or at least name them to return to at another time?
4. What's at stake if you let yourself grow (or stay) cold in this season?

TODAY'S AFFIRMATION

I am loved by the God who created the universe, the same God who is generous with His emotions and awake to His own desires and longings for those He loves. I refuse to grow cold to His love, healing, or hope, and I want to stay warm to His plans, path, and people. I break ties with stoic and detached living, and I ask Him to help me process the moments and decisions that led me here. My awareness of my emotions is not a liability, my hope for healing is not in vain, and I'm committed to keeping my heart soft for whatever is next, in Jesus's name.

Watch Your Words

The tongue has the power of life and death,
and those who love it will eat its fruit.

Proverbs 18:21

Our church has a class called The Way of the Bright. It's our version of a membership class, but we call it an ownership class instead, since we're not a club people join but a church where we all own the mission. We take nine weeks twice a year to talk through how we want to shine the light of Jesus in our city by mirroring God in our creativity, in our hospitality and community, and in the way we use our words.

Each week, there is homework: simple tasks people can do to practice the way of the bright. For the week on words, or speaking life, we do an exercise where everyone has to write a letter or note of encouragement to themselves. During one round, I was feeling a little smug—maybe even a little prideful—and I didn't want to do the homework. I teach the session! I know the material backward and forward. I was also in a pretty rough season of discouragement, and I thought I had graduated from such an exercise. But the Holy Spirit convicted me, and I ended up writing the letter.

I was astounded to find that the short encouragement I spoke to my own soul worked. From somewhere in my spirit, I was able to come up with the exact words I needed to hear. Ironically, this made me feel even more smug and prideful. I began asking myself questions like these:

How come no one else encourages me like this?

Why aren't others as generous with their words as I am?

As He often does, God gently corrected my heart again. And I felt this truth resounding against my own rumblings of frustration: The words of life, encouragement, and hope that I was able to speak over my own soul were more effective than anyone else's because I am deeply acquainted with my own defeat, lies, discouragement, and fears. I have the authority to call up my own spirit in a way that others can't because I am the one closest to my own pain.

I can speak life over myself in ways no other person can.

The power of life and death is in the tongue, and in the midst of our heartbreak, burnout, and brokenness, we have every excuse to speak every word of dread, anger, bitterness, and anxiety that comes to our mind. We have an excuse, and probably even permission from people who love us and feel compassion toward us. But that doesn't mean it will help us feel better.

We will eat the fruit of our words. Consider that those words could instead be words of life, planted in hope for the season ahead.

I never advocate stuffing down our emotions or pretending everything is fine. We are trying to warm up, not freeze our spirits or souls. One way we can begin to let God care for us is by being honest about what hurts, what's hard, and where the pain is piercing us. Alongside that brutal honesty, what if we also spoke words of truth and hope over our lives? What if we experienced our anger without sinning? What if we spoke about those who have hurt us like they're also image bearers of God? What if, instead of declaring that it will always be this way, we prophetically praised God for the relief that we desperately need? What if we were the loudest ones declaring that God is using and will use this pain for our good and His glory?

And here's the real kicker: What if the people around us followed our lead?

I believe that many of us—even those of us who are desperate for someone to come and speak light into the dark seasons we're in—will find ourselves more encouraged by our communities after they see us daring to use words of life instead of death.

And whether anyone else joins in or not, we will have used our words, the most cellular and spiritual form of obedience we have access to, to declare healing and hope where we need it most.

If you are feeling completely lost about where to start, let me help you. Here are a few phrases you can use right now to speak truth over your life:

My pain is not the absence of His presence, love, or favor.

The mercy and compassion of God is coming toward me, even if people are moving away from me.

God will not waste my pain. He will use it to grow me and to help me comfort others and give Him glory.

God will never leave me or forsake me.

God is near to the brokenhearted.

Hope in Jesus does not put me to shame. I can hope boldly, knowing that He will accomplish His good purposes for me.

My present troubles, though difficult, are fleeting. God will wipe away every tear in eternity.

Suffering leads to perseverance, perseverance leads to greater character, and increased character gives me hope.

REFLECTION QUESTIONS

1. What is a negative phrase or refrain that you've found yourself repeating in this season? Where does that thought come from, and does it sound like God?
2. What verses or biblical truths might most empower you today?
3. How could you invite others to speak life over you and also over themselves?
4. What do you stand to lose if you keep speaking death?

TODAY'S AFFIRMATION

Life and death are in the power of my tongue. I may not be able to change my circumstances, I may not be able to shift my life away from pain, hardship, or fatigue, but I have the authority and the opportunity to speak life. I won't wait for others to encourage me. I'll use the Spirit of God that raised Jesus from the dead and the words of life that are waiting for me in His Word to declare healing and hope over my soul and situation. I am a life speaker, I am made in the image of God, and I will use my native language of light to fight the darkness that surrounds me.

DAY 4

We Can Do Hard Things

> I know what it is to be in need, and I know what it is to have plenty. I have learned the secret of being content in any and every situation, whether well fed or hungry, whether living in plenty or in want. I can do all this through him who gives me strength.
>
> Philippians 4:12–13

I have this dream—some might even call it a delusion—that I am the most adaptable person I know. That I find structure, victory, purpose, and beauty in the midst of any situation. I want to believe that if I were dropped out of a helicopter and into the desert alone right now, I would figure out some way to make it enjoyable and life-giving. I wouldn't just cope; I would *thrive*.

The problem is, in my actual life, the smallest inconvenience trips me up. My day can get thrown off by one extra family errand and often leaves me on the verge of tears. A random medical bill comes in the mail and I start pacing. I stay up with a sick child and think I know true suffering. I like to imagine I am adaptable, but my actions say otherwise.

Philippians 4:13 is one of the most misquoted passages in the Bible. We slap it on bumper stickers and jerseys and write it in cards to friends, and our intentions are probably good. We want to believe and share the truth that *we can do all things* with God.

But I honestly believe we would gain more from Paul's words when read in context than we do from just a cursory glance.

Philippians is one of the prison epistles, so named because Paul wrote them from jail. But interestingly, when theologians study these books of the Bible, they often make distinctions between Philippians and Paul's other "jail letters," because he wrote this book from an even more precarious position than the others. In it, he seems to foreshadow his death, he fears for his life, and yet, one of the major themes of the letter is joy in suffering.

When we read this passage in context, we see that Paul isn't saying God can help us pass a test, throw a football, host a great fundraiser, or finish grad school. He's not saying God *can't* help us do those things either. Paul is saying, to some degree, that he has lived the worst-case scenario and has found a way to be content in Christ alone. And we can trust his words because Paul was not delusional like I often am. Having been shipwrecked, beaten, and hard pressed on every side, Paul testified to what is actually possible for those who are in Christ.

I don't know if you're like me and inflate your own internal strength until it's time to actually be strong. Or maybe you are (still) like me, and as soon as reality hits, you feel like you got it all wrong and you don't *actually* want to be God's strongest soldier.

Whether we think we're tough or not, whether we feel ready for the hardship we're experiencing or not, this is the question we're all going to have to come to terms with: *Do we believe Jesus is actually enough?*

Do we believe His presence, His power, His strength, His compassion, His grace, and His care for us will be enough when the bottom falls out? Do we believe God is better than the world's best thing? Do we believe that, when we've lost it all, He is truly the prize?

You and I, in our heartbreak, burnout, and brokenness, have been afforded one beautiful question, but it's not a figurative one. This inquiry rings out from where we sit at rock bottom.

Is Jesus enough for us?

Is it Jesus plus happy days that we worship? Is it Jesus plus an easy life that we crave? Is it Jesus plus our perfect plan working that we signed up for when we surrendered our lives to Him? When we hum the worship songs about Him being "everything," our "all," and "enough," do we really mean it?

I believe that, because you picked up this book during a season that has been neither shiny nor easy for you, somewhere at the core of your soul you want to want God more than you want anything else. And you want to let Him wring His glory and your good out of the pain you are currently experiencing.

My hypothesis is this: If we let God transform us in the middle of our trouble, if we hold up our hands and let Him shift our hearts, we will find ourselves, like Paul, able to say, *I can do all things through Christ who strengthens me, even in incredibly hard seasons.*

REFLECTION QUESTIONS

1. How would you have described yourself in the past?
2. What is your typical immediate response when pain, trouble, or strife pops up in your day?
3. Do you find yourself worshiping Jesus plus something else? What is that something else?
4. Are you ready for God to transform you in this season?

TODAY'S AFFIRMATION

I may have been tempted in the past to worship Jesus plus getting my own way or experiencing comfort in my flesh, but I recognize that pursuit as futile and far from fulfilling. I don't need a worldly identity of being strong or seen as strong by others. Instead, when trouble arises and pain pops up in my life, I want to be found saying that I can do all things through Christ who strengthens me. I can do all things through Christ who strengthens me because He is the prize, He is the best part of my life, and He is my Rock and Redeemer. I have everything I need to weather this storm because I have Him. Even on my most blessed and bright day, He will still be the greatest part of my life.

Don't Leave Yourself

> I will not die but live,
> and will proclaim what the LORD has done.
> Psalm 118:17

I have this thing about being left behind.

I don't like it. I don't like the feeling of watching someone walk away from me. I don't think most people do, but I also wonder if the particular way the Lord has written my story has made me experience it with more sentience than the average human.

Being a pastor in a transient town, you get very used to seeing the backs of people as they walk away. Sometimes it's beautiful. Sometimes people aren't leaving but rather are going somewhere else, saying an obedient *yes* to wherever God is calling them next. But even if you are happy for them, you still have to watch them go.

A few years ago, after I'd been pastoring for a few years, after I'd done a good amount of therapy regarding watching people go, after I thought I was mostly healed from this ever-opening wound, someone very dear to me decided to leave, again. They were moving away soon, and the news came out of nowhere. It took the breath out of me. I thought I would be ready to recite truth, speak life over my pain, and send them off well, but I was left with that gnawing feeling once again. That fear, that lie, that undeniable and angry voice rose up from the pit of hell and yelled to my soul, *You are easy to leave. Once people know you, it's not hard for them to walk away.*

But today's breakthrough isn't really about being left; it's about what I learned on that dark day when I stared down brokenness once again.

The same day this person told me they were leaving, shortly after the gut-wrenching conversation, I had to take my son to work at Chick-fil-A. The news of this leaving was fresh and raw, and my husband offered to drive my son to work since he knew I was in a really fragile place. I declined his polite suggestion and distracted myself by catching up with my eldest as I drove him to work. But on the way back, I was ready to have it out with God.

Audibly and awkwardly, I growled into the empty car from the driver's side: "I hate being left."

At that point in my journey, I had heard a million gentle platitudes about how God would never leave me . . . and I believed them . . . but that day, as I drove away from my son, it wasn't hitting. So I just kept telling God out loud on the drive home, "I hate being left," as I gripped the steering wheel, letting the tears run down my face.

Friends, what happened next was from the Spirit of God. Rather than the old refrains of truth and encouragement that I was used to speaking over myself during pain, a new truth—a bold declaration—rose from my lips and reverberated in the empty car.

"I'm not going to leave me."

I said it once more for good measure.

"I'm not going to leave me."

I wasn't even quite sure what I meant by it, but the idea was forming edges and becoming more concrete. I was realizing that people could come and go, they could reject me, and they could decide what they thought I was worth and treat me accordingly, but I had a move to play, a determination of my own to make. I could choose to stay with me, no matter how broken I was, no matter how needy I felt, and no matter how much it turned out that I did, in fact, need God and could not do it all on my own.

I could be patient with myself. I could apply God's lavish grace to my own soul. I could commit to stay with me, to see the story of redemption play out in my own life. I could look with perseverant eyes and catch a glimpse of glory in the midst of wild weakness.

Fast-forward a few years. I closed the door behind someone I loved deeply as they walked away from me and rejected any future friendship. The Lord brought back the memory of that day in the car.

I almost heard His audible voice beckoning once again: *Say it again.*

"But I won't leave me."

This time it had a verse attached to it. I didn't know the reference, but I knew enough of the refrain to recite it: "I will not die but live, and will proclaim what the Lord has done" (Ps. 118:17).

I don't know your story. But I know you feel heartbroken, burnt out, and tired enough to ask, alongside me, "What comes next?" And so, I invite you to defiantly declare the same words with me today: *God won't leave me, so neither will I. I will stay to see the healing. I will be patient as I process the pain. I will breathe and live and cry and hope and dream again. I won't leave me. And I'll be grateful I stayed.*

REFLECTION QUESTIONS

1. Do you believe that God loves you and will never leave you? If not, what is keeping you from embracing this truth?
2. Have you ever felt tempted to give up on yourself and your own redemption?
3. What would it look like to decide to be patient with yourself, even in the midst of this pain?

TODAY'S AFFIRMATION

God created me, placed me where I'm at on purpose, and He will bring me to a place of healing and redemption. He will not leave me or forsake me, and I will follow His lead. I will accept His presence, grace, patience, and compassion, even when I don't feel like I can earn it or that others in my life will give it. I will tenaciously survey my life for glimpses of His glory, especially in moments of weakness. I will wait on the Lord, I will bless His name, and I will not walk away from the wonder of His goodness that is right here in my midst and that awaits me in the future.

Stop Rehearsing the Nightmare

Do not be anxious about anything, but in every situation, by prayer and petition, with thanksgiving, present your requests to God. And the peace of God, which transcends all understanding, will guard your hearts and your minds in Christ Jesus.

Philippians 4:6–7

Good things take me by surprise.

I rarely anticipate happy, beautiful things before they happen. I didn't grow up fantasizing about my wedding day or picture holding my first baby before they were born. Instead, I tend to envision the negative things. I picture the bottom falling out. I dream about the worst-case scenario.

Sometimes when we read passages like Philippians 4, we immediately dismiss them as unattainable. How could we possibly not be anxious about *anything*? Did Paul understand what his readers might be up against when he wrote those words? I think he did. When he wrote Philippians, he wrote it from jail. From suffering. From loneliness.

Maybe he understood the difference between experiencing fear and anxiety and choosing to live anxious because we're rehearsing the worst-case scenario.

The Greek word for *anxious* here is *merimnaō*, and it has a complex and beautiful definition that gives us more insight than the English version. *Merimnaō* means to be divided or drawn in opposite directions. The Greek understanding of anxiety was of a divided spirit, being pulled apart in your mind somehow, or "going to pieces."

In your current season of heartbreak, burnout, and brokenness, you are bound to have worries that plague you and fears that follow you. But these worries merely mean you are human. Awake to desire. Created to care.

Here are some questions we need to ask: Are you allowing your mind to be divided? Are you waiting for the other shoe to drop? Are you imagining a future where God is not good, not in control, and does not account for you?

To worry is to be human.

But in the midst of hardship, we can choose to stop replaying our worst nightmares. We can take our thoughts captive and submit them to Christ.

One reason I appreciate Paul so much is because he doesn't just tell us what to stop doing; he gives us a little replacement therapy. Instead of excusing and encouraging a divided mind, we have another option. We can pray. We can tell God what we need. We can pour our hearts out before Him.

What's wild is that, when I do this, when I actually pray (not just talk about praying or think about praying), His Word proves true. I feel His peace. I feel protection over my mind and my heart. I find myself able to stop picturing the worst that could happen.

It's funny; all those painful, horrible, heartbreaking seasons never happened the way I pictured. The phone calls that have broken my heart have come out of nowhere. The defeated seasons of fatigue cropped up when I was least expecting them. Not only did my anxious, divided mind fail to help me predict the pain that was headed my way, but it didn't make me any stronger.

And it didn't prepare me for the presence of God in those moments. My nightmares never included His steadfast love beside me in the darkness.

Choosing to constantly fear the worst doesn't prepare you for it. Instead, it cripples your faith, weakens your hope, and leaves you cowering in the corner, hoping your dreams don't come to fruition.

I like to say I'm not a dreamer, but the capacity to imagine pain is obviously well within my reach. So, what if, instead of living with divided minds and continuing to be victims of our anxious imaginations, we were to pray? What if we were to picture God's healing and imagine all the good that could be bringing healing our way?

REFLECTION QUESTIONS

1. Would you consider yourself a dreamer? Why or why not?
2. What is the worst-case scenario you're imagining about your current season? Confess it to God and ask Him to protect your mind and heart.
3. Does your mind feel divided now? How so?

4. What's the best thing that could happen? How could God move on your behalf? What might healing look like?

TODAY'S AFFIRMATION

I am a dreamer. I can partner with God to hope for a vision of healing in my life. I haven't been given a spirit of fear but one of power, love, and self-control. And I will use the authority that I have to draw a line in the sand today. No longer will I rehearse nightmares and partner with the enemy of my soul. My mind is not divided; it is devoted to Jesus and His kingdom. This season of pain does not mean His presence or power has been removed from me. He will not leave me or forsake me. And He promises that the peace of God will guard my mind and my heart until Christ's return. I come into agreement and alignment with that truth now, in the name of Jesus.

(Don't) Make It Make Sense

> There is a time for everything . . .
> a time to mourn and a time to dance.
> Ecclesiastes 3:1, 4

Recently, our family experienced a trifecta of trauma with a sprinkle of burnout and fatigue lightly dusted on top.

It started with my husband's mental health crisis. Out of nowhere, the most stable and peace-filled man I knew was struggling with anxiety and panic. He couldn't sleep, couldn't be alone, couldn't do his job. We attacked the onslaught spiritually and physically, with wisdom and prayer and by getting outside help. He's different now, but he's better. That pain shifted us, made us softer, and God grew us through it, but I still can't tell you why it happened. He had been taking copious vitamins, taking days off, and seeing a therapist before. He was doing all the things you do when you don't want to have a breakdown, and yet break down he did.

Next, the big grief. The one we never could have seen coming. The one we'll be healing from for a long time to come. The one that makes us long for heaven.

My stepdad, Gibson, the kinsman redeemer of our family, lover of history, and backbone of gentle compassion for us, died after complications from surgery. We were devastated. We *are* devastated. Our very close-knit family clung to one another when we could and then fell apart separately when we needed to. We have mourned and wailed, and we know we are going to miss him for the rest of our lives.

The final tent pole of the trifecta of trauma was private. A pain, a breaking, and a heartache that I wish wasn't mine to hold so close. And since it was on the heels of those other two incredibly gut-wrenching realities, I just wasn't ready. I don't know that we are ever ready to have our hearts ripped out, but this one really wrecked me. And, as I write this, it's still going on. I'm in that part of the pain where I wake up and work, love, lead, parent, and try to live, all while my heart feels broken.

And speaking of enduring while you're sad or scared, this is where the sprinkles come in. During this six-month span of sorrow my family walked through, we had four books come out among us, we were all pastoring and leading churches, and we had to lead our teams and families through the trauma with us. Many of you know this feeling: You can't just stop. You can't just not show up. You can bend, you can go slower, you can take breaks, but ultimately, you have to keep living and leading, even when you feel like your life is falling apart.

In the midst of us showing up in our pain, a pattern emerged.

People would ask, in varying levels of gentleness or curiosity, "How did this happen?"

"Do you know what caused Nick's panic attacks?"

"Did you pray during them? Recite verses?"

"Was he getting enough sleep?"

"Had you two been fighting?"

"Do you mind me asking what went wrong during the surgery?"

"Were there signs?"

"How did this happen?"

My mom was the first one who was able to name why people ask *why*. Whether they know it or not, whether they consciously realize they're doing it, people ask why and how because they want to make sure they are safe from experiencing the pain you are in. As soon as she said it, I realized that I have done it my whole life as well; I've tried to trace the steps that landed someone in brokenness so that I could tiptoe around those potholes myself.

But here's the problem: Most of the time, you can't make it make sense.

Pain is present because we live in a fallen world.

Bodies groan under the weight of stress and their environment.

Surgeries that should be textbook turn into trauma.

Cars crash on sunny days without traffic.

People hurt you, even when you're sure you loved them the best you could.

We stub our toes.

We get tired.

We are human, we live under the effects of the fall, and we can't always make pain make sense. We can't blame ourselves, we can't write a map for others to avoid the predicament we find ourselves in, and sometimes we're not even sure how to get out ourselves, so we just keep showing up, grieving, loving, leading, and letting God take care of us.

In your heartbreak, burnout, and brokenness, you might be tempted to say, *this* is what God is doing. *This* is the meaning of the harmful thing I'm experiencing. *This* is what I could have done better. *This* is the purpose of my pain.

But if God is as good and as big as we believe He is, we may not be able to figure Him out entirely. And we may run the risk of putting words or purposes in His mouth that He has never spoken. Moreover, we may miss out on His compassion and care for us if we don't pause long enough to realize that He is coming toward us, heartbroken over our heartbreak. He's a good Dad, who never wants to see His kids in pain, and the more we try to make it make sense, the easier it is for us to forget that.

One day, we may look back in hindsight and say, "I can see *one* of the (million) things He was doing in my life by letting me walk through that." But today is probably not that day.

REFLECTION QUESTIONS

1. Have you been tempted to trace or track how others landed in a season of brokenness?
2. Do you find comfort in knowing God is doing many things to bring purpose and redemption out of your pain?
3. What does it look like for you to keep showing up as you receive His care in the middle of this heartbreak, burnout, or brokenness?

TODAY'S AFFIRMATION

I am a beloved child of God. While I live under the effects of a fallen world, in the midst of sin and brokenness, I am still held and cared for by the God who created and sustains the universe. He will bring purpose to my pain. He will not waste it. He will use it for my good, for the comfort of others, and for His glory—but that is His work to accomplish, not my own. I don't have to make my pain make sense because His ways are higher than mine, and His thoughts are purer than mine. I relinquish my tendency to search out how I got here or to figure out how I'll ever heal. My Father will take care of me.

The Grace of Grief

You then, my son, be strong in the grace that is in Christ Jesus.

2 Timothy 2:1

We belonged to a church years ago that, despite being pretty significant in size, still found ways to feel like a tight-knit community.

One example is that, on Sunday mornings, we had a brief moment for people to share "evidences of God's grace." At the time, each service had around four to five hundred people, but we would pause before worship or teaching each Sunday, and the floor would be open to let people share.

I loved that practice. I loved that they called it "evidences of God's grace." But I wonder if we don't often lose sight of what we mean when we say "grace"—that is, until we're in a difficult or devastating season.

I came of age in Christian community during the early 2000s, and I remember how often I heard sermons trying to unpack the difference between God's grace and His mercy. Despite my familiarity with the topic, and despite attending seminary and being a pastor, I sometimes still forget. I forget just how majestic and beautiful God's grace and mercy truly are—until I am desperate for them.

In my spiritual upbringing, the quick definitions offered to me were something like this: Mercy is *not* getting what you deserve (punishment for your sins), and grace is *getting* what you don't deserve (the unmerited favor of God).

And, of course, like most spiritual "definitions," the concepts take on a wildly different meaning when we realize we actually need them.

That's what happened to me with grace during my most recent season of grief.

I had lived years being able to tune out, or at the least turn down, the song of grace in my life. I could hum along, I could say the right words, I could pretend that I thought I was getting things I didn't deserve, but life and time were lulling me into the false belief that I *did* deserve them. I *did* deserve my family because I worked hard to cultivate the community within our home. I *did* deserve my job because I had put in the time needed to build my career. I *did* deserve our church because we were honest and hardworking leaders. I *did* deserve my friends because I showed up for them and was intentional about pouring into our relationships.

Would I have said any of this out loud? Never. But did I believe it nonetheless? Sadly, yes.

Peering past the grief, if we look hard enough, we can often find grace in these times:

When life starts to fall apart.

When we lose someone we love.

When we realize our carefully laid plans are still leading to pain.

When we are abandoned.

When we disappoint someone.

When we are exhausted.

When we remember that we still need God just as desperately as we did at the point of salvation, we are confronted with the most beautiful and brutal truth: If we are not responsible or to blame for every bad thing that happens in our lives, then we cannot take credit for every good thing that God has given us either.

For most of us, as we experience hardship, there is a period when we look inward and ask, *How did I get here? What could I have done differently?* And those questions are holy and humble. But there is also deep humility and wisdom in surrendering when you realize that none of us can anesthetize our entire lives from hardship. Pain is headed our way because we live under the effects of a fallen world, whether we've made every right decision or not.

And so, if we don't want to be buried by shame or stuck in a pattern of feeling humiliated by the pain that surrounds us, we must be humbled by the grace of the good and the beautiful, admitting we don't actually deserve or earn any of it on our own. If we can't take all the credit for the hard, then we can't take all the credit for the holy.

There is a grace in seasons of grief because pain reminds us how much we need God. Pain also emphasizes the beauty of every little miracle, every little gift, and every little grace.

And what's more, at our lowest, when we feel like we have nothing to offer the Lord or the people around us—when our pain has left us seemingly useless—we are reminded of the grace that God draws near to us anyway.

I love this line that Paul slips into 2 Timothy: "Be strong in the grace . . ." Speaking of the subtle and important differences between grace and mercy, I recently learned the subtle difference between 1 and 2 Timothy. Both are letters from Paul to Timothy, a man Paul had invested in deeply and was raising up to lead in his wake. But in 2 Timothy, Paul is a little more desperate because he believes he is going to die soon. This letter is effectively his last will and testament, his parting words to his partner in the gospel.

Be strong in . . . wisdom?

Be strong in . . . leadership?

Be strong in . . . your teaching skills?

Be strong in grace.

Be strengthened by this knowledge: God is giving you what you don't deserve—His unmerited favor and kindness—when you deserve it the least. God is coming toward you, seeing you, holding you, and sustaining you. Be strong in the knowledge that you didn't earn it, and be freed from the shame you feel when it doesn't go your way. Amen? Amen.

REFLECTION QUESTIONS

1. Have you gotten into the habit of believing that you earn the beauty and hardship in your life?
2. What is still true about you in this difficult season? What is still true about God?
3. What evidence of God's grace do you currently see in your life?
4. What do you think it would look like for you to be "strong in grace"?

TODAY'S AFFIRMATION

The God of the universe is coming toward me with healing, help, and wholeness because He loves me and made a way for me. Whether the hardship I'm experiencing is my "fault" or not, He is not shaming me or moving away from me, because His mercy forever endures for His children. My life is filled with evidence of His grace, and I will be intentional about seeing those graces, speaking them, and giving Him glory for the ways He shows up for me. In the name of Jesus, I resist the temptation to boast about the life I've built or to wallow in shame about my season of pain. Instead, I will live strong in grace, aware of His kindness toward me in every season.

DAY 9

Thank God for the Fleas

Rejoice always, pray continually, give thanks in all circumstances; for this is God's will for you in Christ Jesus.

1 Thessalonians 5:16–18

A friend reminded me recently about the book *The Hiding Place* by Corrie ten Boom.

Corrie was a Christian survivor of a concentration camp during WWII, who, alongside her family, helped many Jewish people escape the Nazis by hiding them in her home before she was ultimately captured herself. *The Hiding Place* is the story of how her family fought to survive, but it's also a story of how they fought to give God glory in the midst of unspeakable trauma.

Near the end of the book, when Corrie and her family have suffered exceeding loss and heartache, after they have grasped continually to give God glory, there is a narrative about gratitude that is absolutely life-shifting. One night, while Corrie and her sister Betsie are on a quest to choose deep spiritual gratitude in the midst of their pain, to find something to thank God for even when it feels impossible, Betsie encourages Corrie to thank God for the fleas that have infested their barracks.

Corrie says, "Betsie, there's no way even God can make me grateful for a flea."

Betsie replies, "'Give thanks in *all* circumstances.' . . . Fleas are part of this place where God has put us."[1]

As Corrie tells the story, the girls discover days later that the reason they have been given so much "freedom" in their barracks, to read the Bible and share it with others and to go unharmed by guards, is because no one in charge of the concentration camp wanted to be exposed to the fleas.[2] The fleas had kept them safe, allowed them to experience Christian fellowship in a seemingly godless place, and allowed them to advance the gospel in the midst of their own pain.

This story, along with the rest of the book, changed me and gave me hopeful eyes to look at the landscape of my own hardest seasons, scouring for any evidence of helpful "fleas."

Thank You, God, that this person left and for how that might have been Your protection.

Thank You, God, for this fatigue that is helping me experience Your grace and power in a new way.

Thank You, God, for the comfort I'm receiving in this trial, which equips me to comfort others.

Thank You, God, for the car breaking down.

Thank You, God, for the unkind word that led me to Your Word for comfort.

---

1. Corrie ten Boom with Elizabeth and John Sherrill, *The Hiding Place*, deluxe ed. (Chosen: 2023), 210.

2. Ten Boom, *Hiding Place*, 220.

Thank You, God, for this busy day, in which I feel like I can't get a break.

Thank You, God, for using every single detail of my life for my ultimate good and Your glory.

Thank You, God, for the fleas.

Toxic positivity is defined as the act of suppressing or invalidating negative emotions in favor of a false sense of happiness and satisfaction. Another related phrase is *spiritual bypassing*, which is defined as the tendency to use spiritual practices to avoid facing difficult, painful, or unresolved issues. I hope you know by now that I wouldn't advocate for either, and I don't believe the apostle Paul or Jesus would either.

Toxic positivity tells us to pretend that the fleas don't matter, to pretend that you like them or enjoy them, which would mean missing out on receiving the comfort and care our Father longs to give us. Spiritual bypassing would say that the act of gratitude can help us escape or evade the pain of our circumstances, that if we're thankful for the fleas, maybe we won't even feel their bites on our bodies.

But wild spiritual gratitude in the midst of pain and loss says, I will not pretend that this is not hard. I will not somehow transcend this difficulty by determination or by saying that it doesn't really matter. I will grieve. I will process. I will go to God for the compassion that He pours out, and I'll let my tears fall at His feet. I will be honest with Him when I feel like I can't keep going, and at the same time, I will relentlessly search out His mercy.

We don't *have* to choose faith-filled, audacious gratitude; we *get* to. We don't *have* to thank God for the fleas, but we *get* to. Because it's good for our hearts. Because it helps us agree with the kingdom truth that God's kingdom comes when His will is done. And His will for our lives is done when we rejoice *always*, pray *continually*, and give thanks in *all circumstances*.

REFLECTION QUESTIONS

1. Have there been times in your past when you've expressed audacious gratitude and it shifted your perspective?
2. What are the "fleas" in your current situation?
3. Why do you think it might be important for you to express gratitude in the midst of your own hardship? How will it shift your spirit or life?
4. Is there anyone you need to invite into your expression of thanks to God, as a community activity, the way Corrie and Betsie thanked Him together?

TODAY'S AFFIRMATION

I don't have to rejoice in my suffering, pray in the midst of my pain, or give thanks in this circumstance, but I want to. I want all of God's will, kingdom, hope, and healing that is available to me. I want to draw near to Him. I want to come into alignment with the intimacy that Jesus has purchased for me on the cross. I want all of His care, and I want all of the comfort that is available to me. I want to walk with God in the midst of my heartbreak, burnout, and brokenness. I want to thank God for the fleas—not because I have to but because I get to. And I know that I will be able to trace His heart and His hand in my life when I use this spiritual practice of gratefulness, even now.

DAY 10

How Do You Want This to Go?

> I have fought the good fight, I have finished the race, I have kept the faith.
>
> 2 Timothy 4:7

I always say that my daughter, Glory, woke me up to life.

She had just turned four years old when she had her first seizure, a grand mal that should have left her unable to walk or talk. The seizure came out of nowhere—no prior family history, no signs other than some grumpy toddler behavior—and it lasted hours, despite the copious amounts of antiseizure medication she received in the hospital. I said the seizure should have left her unable to walk or talk, but the truth is, it did rob her of those capacities in the early days. Only a miracle of wild proportions is what enables her to do both today.

The story of what happened that morning isn't funny, but our family sometimes tells it in a funny way—at least the part about what I did when fight-or-flight failed me and all I could do was freeze. I stood holding her, shrieking and screaming, while my husband called an ambulance and packed up our boys, instinctively knowing they'd need to stay with family that night. I just stood there, shrieking.

Later, in the ER, I realized I was still in my pajamas, and I sat holding her feet, watching them twitch, not knowing what to do or how to help. It was like being in a nightmare where I couldn't scream, except in this situation, I couldn't pray, talk, or even cry. I just sat there, frozen.

My mom arrived at the hospital soon after we did—probably *too soon*, given that she lived two hours away at the time. She brought me a toothbrush, and as I was brushing, she gently peppered me with questions about what kind of medicine they'd tried, what the plan was, and what she could do to help.

I mumbled something, still barely coherent, as my mom laid her strong hand on my ice-cold arm, interrupting my brushing.

"Jess. You're going to have to fight."

Internally, something shifted in me that day. I woke up from what felt like a decade-long fog, where I had been doing nothing but reacting, responding, and following the lead of whoever was the loudest in front of me. I hadn't been cultivating the situations or seasons I was in; I had just been numbly inheriting whatever drifted in front of me. I had not been awake.

In retelling the story, I guess I should credit my daughter Glory and my mom for helping me wake up that day. I know they would both tell me to also give honor to the real slumber assailant, the Holy Spirit, who raised Jesus Christ from the dead.

My tendency when things get hard is just to receive them. And I'm not talking about shock. I'm talking about resignation.

I am not a catastrophizer.

One day, a friend introduced me to three questions that I now allow God to ask of me in the middle of hard seasons, painful moments, and stretches of prolonged fatigue:

How do you want this to go?

How do you want to have shown up and handled it when it's over?

What story do you want to tell when this is finished?

At the time, my friend was referencing a really difficult period of stress and busyness, but her question woke me up in the same way that my mom's words had that day in the hospital.

What if you didn't just resign yourself to the story being sad and the road being long? What if you didn't just accept that "this is just the way it is"? What if you didn't just let this heartbreak, burnout, and brokenness happen to you, but you decided to see your authority and capacity in this season?

We touched on the context of 2 Timothy in Day 8, the finality and passion of Paul's last letter, his will and testament, and his passing of the torch. In light of that, the words he writes at the end of his life, with such assurance, read to me like this (in my very unholy paraphrase): *I stayed awake. I didn't become the victim of suffering. I became the victor. I fought for God's glory. I fought with the end in mind, and it worked. I knew how I wanted this to go, and I'm grateful to report—it has been good.*

We've spent these last ten days letting God care for us in the midst of our pain. And these days have not been a waste. They have not been counterproductive or self-indulgent. We could spend a thousand days letting God care for us as we experience the brokenness of this earth, and as we move forward, we won't stop letting Him care for us. We won't pretend that there aren't wounds to attend to. But for the rest of our time together, we will start asking:

How do we want this to go?

How do we want to have shown up and handled it when it's over?
What story do we want to tell when this is finished?
What comes next?

REFLECTION QUESTIONS

1. When you finish this devotional, what do you want to be able to say is true?
2. Are there any ways that you are resigned to pain when you could be fighting for healing?
3. Do you feel too tired to fight? If so, that's okay. Talk to God about it.
4. Is there anything you're scared of in regard to moving forward?

TODAY'S AFFIRMATION

I am not just a victim of a broken world. I am not just my pain. My identity is not completed in the suffering, fatigue, or heaviness of my present season. By the power that raised Jesus Christ from the grave, I have been made and called victorious by the King of Kings and the Lord of Lords. I have been given spiritual gifts: wisdom, insight, power that's made perfect in weakness, patience, compassion, and the capacity to hope in future healing. This heartache is real, but so is Christ's light in my darkness. The light is breaking in, and it's shining hope on everything the darkness stole. I can't wait to see what comes next.

Shame Off You

> So do not be ashamed of the testimony about our Lord or of me his prisoner. Rather, join with me in suffering for the gospel, by the power of God.
>
> 2 Timothy 1:8

I was in the back row at church, sobbing.

Our family was in the hardest season we'd ever lived through. As I write this, there is a part of me that wants to condescendingly pat past-me on the top of her head and say, "You ain't seen nothing yet, sweetie!" But mostly, I feel so much compassion for this messy gal, who was snotting her way through a worship service.

Our family had unintentionally relocated. An intended two-week pit stop to fundraise for our future church plant had come to a screeching halt after a freak accident coupled with lapsed health insurance had drained our finances and stolen our fervor. Everyone was asking us, "What's next?" and we didn't have the faintest idea.

We were hopping between staying with my mom and stepfather and staying with my sister and brother-in-law, all of whom were massively gracious to welcome us—but none of their homes or lives were set up to permanently accommodate our family of five. Would we still plant a church? Was God telling us to pause? Had we ever been ready in the first place? Should we just give up? Where would we live? What would we do? What was next?

I'd gone to church that night alone, slunk in the back door, and let myself crumble in the back row. I honestly thought I was pretty incognito until I realized there were a handful of older women surrounding me, praying for me, and interceding on my behalf. They didn't know what was wrong, but they wanted to support me in prayer, and I just let myself keep on crying without explaining. The story was too much. We were too much. We were failures before we even began.

Eventually, the music ended, the lights came on, and people began filing past my red, tearstained cheeks and piles of tissues. The women stayed until the room was mostly empty and the noise had died down. They kept their firm hands on my back and my hands filled with fresh tissue until finally, one of them asked, "Did a boy hurt your feelings?"

If my fear and confusion hadn't been so raw, I might have laughed. And if my shame hadn't been so deep, I might have corrected them. But instead, I just said, "Yeah . . . something like that."

On the way home, as I processed my intimate encounter with those women at church, the thought occurred to me: *A boy did hurt my feelings. A God-man. Jesus called us into ministry, left us when we needed Him most, and now we have no hope. Now we look like fools. Now we feel like failures. But we were only trying to give Him glory.*

But I now have the perspective and healing that can only be found in hindsight.

Not planting that church led us to a season of recovery, wholeness, and abundance that is still pouring out of us today. I know now that, a few months after that, because of our dire financial straits, I would start an online shop that would eventually become the small business that has funded our ministry for over a decade. I know now that the mommy blog I was writing in the midst of our "failure," with musings about Scripture and strategy, would turn into a career in publishing. I know now that because we didn't plant the church we planned to in Boston, we would be able to plant the church we were supposed to plant in Charleston.

I know now that God had not left me; He was holding me.

I know now that what looked like our greatest breakdown was the beginning of a breakthrough.

I know now that I had nothing to be ashamed of as I cried in that back row; life was scary, the future was unknown, and money was absolutely nonexistent.

All I knew then was that I was embarrassed.

And that's why, once again, I am so thankful for the apostle Paul.

Because in a situation where he could have easily been humiliated about the perceived "failure" of his ministry and felt shame about his circumstances, he reminds Timothy of some powerful truths:

Do not be ashamed of God.

Do not be ashamed of me.

Suffering is not a potential path for the unlucky, it is a guaranteed reality for all of us.

And so, I vote that you and I use our precious spiritual, emotional, mental, and physical energy to begin healing rather than sitting in the shame that Jesus died to save us from.

Shame off you in your brokenness and burnout.

Whether you caused your present circumstances or not, "therefore, there is now no condemnation for those who are in Christ Jesus" (Rom. 8:1). Amen? Amen.

REFLECTION QUESTIONS

1. On a scale of 1–10, how much shame do you feel about your current circumstances?
2. What do you think Jesus would say to you about your shame?
3. Is there any blame you've put on God that you need to confess right now?
4. What would it look like for you to move forward, away from shame?

TODAY'S AFFIRMATION

I refuse to let the enemy's lies of shame be louder than God's voice of victory in my life. I refuse to advocate for the devil by reasoning out my responsibility and staying defeated in disgrace. The mistakes of my past and my future cannot separate me from the love of God, so I will own them and move forward, receiving the grace that is mine for the taking. I refuse to cower in shame about the pain and trauma that have happened to me against my will either. I will remember that suffering is the path of gospel-minded people, and I will boast in the goodness and glory of God while I await the healing and wholeness that are eternally mine in Christ Jesus.

DAY 12

The Connective Tissue of Wounds

He heals the brokenhearted
and binds up their wounds.
Psalm 147:3

I have this weird beauty pageant injury.

I hope you laughed when you read that line because I laughed typing it.

If someone says they have an "old soccer injury," you assume they were pretty good at soccer. If someone says they have a "recurring running injury," you mostly infer they have put in a good amount of miles.

I have a beauty pageant injury, but we should be abundantly clear: I haven't been in multiple beauty pageants, and I certainly did not excel during my short stint as a contestant.

I was in one pageant.

I volunteered to be in it, meaning no one nominated me.

Or maybe I nominated myself?

And I came nowhere close to winning.

But the day I was in said pageant, someone opened a very large door onto my toe, absolutely mangling my toenail. It probably required direct care, but because it was an hour before this potentially life-changing event (no one's life changed—certainly not mine), I stuffed my gnarly looking foot into a four-inch heel and hoped for the best.

And it has never been the same since.

It hurts when I run.

It hurts when the weather is weird.

It throbs on planes, which I'm sure has something to do with the pressure in the air.

One night, I had to leave a concert because it was hurting so badly that I couldn't even sit quietly and listen to jazz music.

As I write this, I am realizing that I should probably get this thing looked at.

But we grow accustomed to our wounds, fond of their familiarity and impartial to the pain they continually inflict. That is, until there is another injury, perhaps completely unrelated, and we become increasingly aware of the interconnectivity of our wounds.

Chances are, what's hurting you right now isn't an isolated issue. That heartbreak, burden, or heaviness is pressing in on the pains of your past, the ones that were easier to stuff down and gloss over.

Maybe your spouse has been unfaithful and it reminds you of when your dad left. Your child has a terrifying medical diagnosis and you realize you never started trusting God again after your friend died. An unexpected bill comes in the mail and suddenly you pick up the scent of secondhand clothes, the only ones your family could afford when you were growing up.

Your boss sends back a report for a second try and you wonder if he found out you got rejected from every business school you applied to. Your friend asks you for a favor on your day off, and it should be no big deal, but you have yet to recover from the wild fatigue of last year.

This is why we must take the time to heal.

Because life will keep coming at us with new trials and fresh challenges. And wouldn't it be wonderful if we weren't all walking around wounded, limping from injuries that should have long since healed?

I wish that, on that warm October night in 2001, I had realized that paying attention to the state of my demolished toe was actually more urgent than a pageant I was never going to win. At the very least, I wish I would have cared enough to wear some flats or see the doctor the next day.

But more than that, I wish that you and I would value our present health and our future wholeness enough to take the time to heal. I wish we would trust God enough to hold up our broken hearts to Him with as much hope as we can muster and ask, "Can You help this?" I wish we would be brave enough to keep going back for help, even when it feels futile. I wish we would trust Him enough, just like little kids, to expose the tender wounds that we have been hiding or trying to mend on our own.

I wish we would see healing for the courageous, Spirit-empowered, generous option of leadership and love that it is. I wish we would feel comfortable taking up space in the throne room of grace while our Great High Priest ministers to our hearts.

Because just like many wounds can be connected to one another, our healing is also interconnected.

And when He binds up one area of our broken heart, we'll notice freedom and authority released in other areas of our lives. Take the time you need to let God heal your broken heart, and pay attention to the rest of the release that heads your way.

REFLECTION QUESTIONS

1. What hurts *right now*? What is the wound of today?
2. What is that pain connected to? Memories or unhealed moments from the past?
3. What, if anything, has kept you from healing up till now? Has it been shame? Lack of time or community?
4. Do you believe that anything can keep you from healing this time? And if so, why do you see God as limited in power in this particular circumstance?

TODAY'S AFFIRMATION

God's Word may refer to my suffering as light and momentary in relation to eternity, but my healing will be anything but. While it may hurt, when God shines a light on my wounds to help bind them, there is no shame, no blame, and only hope ahead. My healing is worthy of time and attention because it's one way I'll experience God's nearness and power in my life.

Forgive God

Don't you see how wonderfully kind, tolerant, and patient God is with you? Does this mean nothing to you? Can't you see that his kindness is intended to turn you from your sin?

Romans 2:4 NLT

I started my very first paid ministry job at the ripe age of twenty, and one day, the pastor who was in charge of leading me sat me down to discuss my tone.

He was so gracious, so patient, so wise, and what he said changed my life and work forever.

"Jess, everyone has a 'ministry tool belt.' God has given you multiple tools to do your work or to get your point across. I'm afraid you only know how to reach for the hammer."

Fast-forward two decades later to where I sat with a friend, remembering that conversation. I was searching through my mental ministry tool belt for any other device I could pull out. *God, give your girl a paintbrush! Or a very tiny, gentle screwdriver. Please help me not show up as the hammer today.*

My friend was sharing some of what was going on in her life at the moment, what she was feeling and how angry she was at God.

I want to pause here and say that, for years, I have advocated that expressed anger is still intimacy. I'm an advocate of talking to God about our disappointments and frustrations, asking Him "why" with passion, or even just whispering to the sky, "I don't understand what You're doing."

But this situation was different. I had a gut feeling about what my friend needed to hear next. I don't suggest uttering the following few words unless you have a very close relationship with the person you're addressing. I told her, "I think you might need to repent."

We went on to talk for another hour about how God had actually been miraculously showing up in her life recently, and I had some behind-the-scenes knowledge to encourage this. I knew about some money that had shown up anonymously to help her pay her bills. I reminded her of how she had only recently recounted His faithfulness in giving her wisdom and insight about different decisions she needed to make. I knew that her fear and defeat were temporarily blinding her from seeing God's goodness, and I felt comfortable enough as her friend to suggest she turn around to see it.

Repentance is just that, turning toward a new way.

It is the intentional shifting of our thoughts that changes our behavior.

I share both of those stories because I think they're both important when we talk about forgiving God. I want you to know that I don't come to you today with a hammer, and I'm not suggesting that you never express your frustration or disappointment with God.

But many of us are aiming our frustration in the wrong place. We have blamed God for this world's brokenness when, in reality, He grieves it more than we ever could. We have doubted God's capacity and power when we haven't been able to see or perceive the whole plan. We have spoken ill of Him, as if He's like us or could ever experience conflicted and unholy motives like we do.

It's not that God can't handle the blame and bitterness coming His way. The real problem when we walk around with unresolved or unprocessed anger toward God is that we miss out on receiving His kindness and patience while we're railing and reeling.

When we write a narrative about Him that is opposite of His character, assuming He wants bad for us, that He is trying to harm us, or that He has forgotten us, we misunderstand and slander His identity. And we begin to live into and make agreements with that false representation, which keeps us from enjoying His presence and power right where we're at.

It is with the most gentle tool in my tool belt—my humbled confession—that I offer this as an option if we believe we need to forgive God: We may need to repent. We may need to apologize for approaching Him as if He's human, fallible, or at fault for the brokenness we're experiencing. We may need to remind our hearts of His goodness, grace, and generous provision toward us. We may need to change our minds, our words, and the way we speak about Him. We may need to get on our knees and return to seeking His face in humble desire. Because He *is* trustworthy. He *is* compassionate toward His kids. And He *will* use our hardship and pain for our good.

This makes forgiving God as simple as turning around.

REFLECTION QUESTIONS

1. How have you blamed God for your present pain?
2. Are the assumptions you're making about His character true and in line with Scripture?
3. What truths could you repeat or affirm to remember what is true about Him?
4. How have you experienced His compassion and patience in this process?

TODAY'S AFFIRMATION

My Father is trustworthy, kind, faithful, and constantly moving toward me in compassion. He does not delight in my suffering, but He is working for my good, even when I cannot see it. His plans for me are for welfare and not for evil, to give me a future and a hope. I am not alone, because God is continually with me and for me, guiding me and guarding me. He goes before me and behind me, He does not miss a detail of my life. He does not forget to care for any of His kids. I am seen, held, and loved, even when I doubt His love for me.

Forgive Them

When you forgive this man, I forgive him, too. And when I forgive whatever needs to be forgiven, I do so with Christ's authority for your benefit, so that Satan will not outsmart us. For we are familiar with his evil schemes.

2 Corinthians 2:10–11 NLT

My fifteen-year-old jokes that he only recently became sentient.

He says that, up until a year ago, he knew he existed and was present in the world, but he wasn't really awake to his emotions, thoughts, or even the reality of his relationships. I appreciate that he's the one who said it and that he's humble enough to admit there was a long period where he wasn't super engaged in our family. I share that as an encouragement as well for any moms of preteen boys who feel like the shallow level of grunts and below-average communication skills are an indicator of bad things to come. It's okay, they just might not be sentient yet.

The thing is, I love that he can identify this because I can remember waking up from a similar stupor in my teens. I remember the first time I realized I'd really hurt someone, that I'd really messed up and been unkind. I'd certainly been unkind before that, but suddenly, I felt the weight of my actions. I remember the first time I truly *missed* someone and imagined a better moment if they had been present. And I have redolent memories of the first time someone hurt me deeply and the first time I thought, *Man . . . I'm never going to get over this.*

That profound perception drops in your stomach like a large stone to the bottom of a murky pit. Whether they meant to or not, whether they knew they hurt you or not, whether they're sorry or not, experiencing emotional harm at the hands of someone else for the first time is an incredibly difficult experience. I remember the immediate switch in my soul, where I went from feeling completely safe to incredibly scared, knowing the way someone else could make me feel and that there was nothing I could do about it.

That very first time we were hurt, we had options, whether we knew it or not. We could respond in defense, anger, or shock. We could pretend that it didn't hurt, or we could lash out or retaliate. We could ask questions, demand answers, or call in outside reinforcements. And now, even still, when we're sinned against, we have options.

And according to Paul, one option is to continue in unforgiveness and therefore be outsmarted by the enemy of our souls.

I can't imagine exactly what the apostle meant when he used this language. But because I have had situations in my life where I've been hurt and responded by withholding forgiveness, I can explain why my decision to do so was a trick, a deception, and a sleight of hand. We think that by holding on to our hurt and anger, by guarding our forgiveness, we are somehow taking care of ourselves. The other person did not care for us, so out of self-protection, we do what is right for ourselves. We will meet our own needs. Only, the unforgiveness ends up poisoning our souls, causing us harm, and keeping us from healing. Meanwhile, the person who hurt us may not even know or care about the impact they have had on our lives.

What's more, a root of unforgiveness can cause us to see ourselves as capable of judging others, as if we are not also at Jesus's feet, in continual need of grace. So, ultimately, when we use a short ruler of compassion for others, we end up turning that same measurement on our own souls.

Here's another pitfall we encounter when we let the enemy convince us to live without forgiveness: We miss the distinction between letting people continually hurt us and releasing them through the act of forgiveness. We falsely believe that forgiveness means accepting someone's faults. Because of this, we see our possibilities as two opposite ends of a spectrum: Don't forgive and take care of ourselves, *or* allow the other person to win and continue potentially harming us.

While the process of forgiveness looks vastly different depending on who we are and what has happened to us, I believe we will find insight when we ask these questions:

How is the enemy trying to outsmart me?

What peace and release is he trying to rob from me?

What would it look like to surrender our right to hold on to an offense, anger, bitterness, or unforgiveness?

I know this about our Father: He's a better communicator than I am. And He will give us the wisdom we need to move forward with grace.

One more note: Maybe you're like me and, over time, as people have hurt you, you've become *less* sentient. Maybe you've become less aware and less sensitive to the vulnerability of being in a relationship with people who are constantly capable of hurting you. Maybe you view this "toughness" as maturity. I wonder if God might want to restore your sensitivity. The aim of our lives cannot be never getting hurt. It's just not realistic. But the aim of our lives *can* be making sure we allow our pain to shift us, grow us, and send us both softly and boldly into whatever is next.

REFLECTION QUESTIONS

1. Where is there unforgiveness in your heart?
2. How has the enemy confused you in the past regarding the meaning of forgiveness and what it should look like in your life?
3. What do you think God is telling you forgiveness looks like in this season?
4. Has your heart grown hard toward people? Have you assumed that spiritual maturity means no longer caring when people hurt you?

TODAY'S AFFIRMATION

I come into alignment with the grace and strength of God my Father and agree that I have access to a phenomenal capacity for compassion and forgiveness. Because I have been forgiven, I can and will extend grace to those who have harmed me, not only because it's how I live into the image of my invisible God but because it's good for my soul. God will give me the courage to release others from the bondage of shame and unforgiveness. God will give me peace that surpasses understanding when I can't achieve resolution, closure, or retaliation. I agree that the Holy Spirit will give me insight into any practical steps I need to walk in full healing and forgiveness, in Jesus's name.

DAY 15

Forgive Yourself

So now there is no condemnation for those who belong to Christ Jesus. And because you belong to him, the power of the life-giving Spirit has freed you from the power of sin that leads to death.

Romans 8:1–2 NLT

It was one of the first verses I memorized as an adult.

I would recite it in clipped phrases, as if constructing a shield around my body and soul: *"Therefore, there is . . . now no . . . condemnation . . . for those . . . who are in . . . Christ Jesus."*

It's hard for me to relate to people who don't think they've ever really screwed up. It's hard for me to understand people who see everyone else as the villain and have never had to look in the mirror knowing they're to blame. It's hard for me to connect with people who have never had to speak these words from Romans 8 over their own soul in a desperate attempt to slow their heartbeat and steady their breath, pleading for it to help them fall asleep in the midst of deep shame.

Sometimes I feel shame because I am truly to blame. Sometimes I feel shame because my humanity has betrayed me and I simply made a mistake. Sometimes I feel shame even though I haven't done anything wrong, except fail to meet someone's arbitrary or unhealthy expectations. Whatever the cause has been, I have known shame. I am well acquainted with my deepest disappointment in life being myself.

It's often easier to approach reconciliation when we're the ones who have been wronged. We need to extend what has been extended to us. We need to mirror and reflect the compassion and grace that our Father has extended to us. But what about the times *we* need forgiveness? How do we forgive ourselves? What does this look like when we are the ones who caused the hurt? One complication here is that most of us are painfully aware of our own intentions and broken desires.

I'm not embarrassed to admit that I love a little reality TV. I think it's a fascinating study of how people really act, including at their worst. My favorite and least favorite thing about reality TV, however, is when people try to excuse their actions by claiming some version of "My intentions were totally good! I never meant to hurt you!"

The problem with making statements like that on reality TV is that viewers like me just witnessed that same person do something diabolical, and their intentions seemed anything but pure. The cameras caught it all. There is no hiding behind a script.

Sometimes I think we're the most skeptical viewers of our own reality show. We know our own motives and how selfish we can get. We know our true intentions and the thoughts that pass through our heads that no one else can hear. We know what we're capable of. And we are often much more aware of the pain and hurt we can cause than we are of our positive traits.

If it's hard to extend grace to a stranger on television, how much harder is it to extend forgiveness to ourselves, knowing what we know? This is where we can be incredibly grateful that it's not our grace, our strength, our saving, or our redemption that does the work. It's all Jesus.

There is therefore now no condemnation for us because the power of the life-giving Spirit has freed us from the power of sin that leads to death. We are not free because we are perfect. We are not free because we meant well. We are not free because we plan to make it up or fix it. We are not free because other people think we're okay. We are not free because we did it right the first time. We are not free because we got defensive and fought for it. We are free because, if we are in Christ Jesus, the same Spirit that raised Him from the grave bears witness over our souls and says condemnation can't touch us.

We can't be condemned because our sins have already been discovered and covered.

Does this freedom lead us to indulge in our flesh and keep messing up? It shouldn't! Rather, it should compel us to move forward and live like we have been freed. It should compel us to keep showing grace to others in the name of Jesus.

We release God from needing our forgiveness because He never did.

We release others by forgiving them the way we want to be forgiven by Christ.

And we release ourselves by receiving God's mercy and reminding ourselves that there is therefore now no condemnation because Christ died for us too.

And now, in the name of Jesus, it feels like we can finally begin to heal.

REFLECTION QUESTIONS

1. When in the past have you felt the deepest shame? How did you handle it?
2. Are there any parts of your identity, past or present, where you are holding on to condemnation?
3. What might the redeeming power of Christ look like in your life if you let it truly take root?
4. How will receiving this message of condemnation-free living help you love others moving forward?

TODAY'S AFFIRMATION

When shame and condemnation threaten to take me out, I will hide under the banner of Jesus. God is not surprised when I need grace. He does not move away from me when He sees my intentions, no matter how sinful they may be. I am not safe because I have done everything right, and I am not secure because I will handle everything well in the future. I am held by a Father who has accounted for me. I am loved by my Friend and Savior, Jesus, who purchased my redemption with His very life. And I am empowered by the Holy Spirit, who cries out "Grace!" on my behalf.

DAY 16

Don't Stop the Grieving

Out of the depths I have cried to You, O Lord;
Lord, hear my voice!
Let Your ears be attentive
To the voice of my supplications.

Psalm 130:1–2 NASB1995

I had a plan for my grief.

In fact, I had the phases outlined. They had titles and everything.

I knew how I wanted the plan to go. First, I would take some time for the initial trauma and shock to boil and burn away. I figured this might take a few weeks. Then, I'd let myself get really low and down about the intense loss, mourning a past, present, and future that had forever shifted. After that, I would focus my attention on those around me, mourning in community, as my family had experienced this pain together. By this phase, I would have my head back on my shoulders, and

I could focus on being there for them. And then, finally, the bitterness would become bittersweet, and I would only have to deal with the occasional prolonged, sweeping moments of sadness washing over me.

I remember telling a friend who had also lost a parent about my plan. We were talking over Zoom, catching up before a work meeting, and I couldn't tell if the internet had paused or what was happening. She had been talking, and then all of a sudden she stopped. She just stared at me.

I checked to make sure she was still with me, and she confirmed with a nod before she replied, "I really hope that works out for you, Jess."

She knew my plan was never going to work.

She had foreknowledge that I didn't: You can't schedule your grief.

I'm not sure what season of life you're in that led you to pick up this book. I'm not sure what grief, brokenness, or heaviness hovers over your heart right now. But I am certain, mostly because of what I've experienced, that if you try to close the lid on grief when you still have grieving to do, you will continually push your healing back further and further. If you try to draw a line in the sand of your soul and say, "No more grieving; we're done here. Pull it together. It's time to move on," you will continually do the opposite.

I have watched enough medical dramas on TV to know this about X-rays: When the scan is displayed on the wall against a lit-up projector and the medical professional examines a bone, they can tell which are fresh breaks and which are ones that never healed. Life, relationships, and walking with God would be much simpler if we could put up a picture of our soul and see which old wounds are still healing under the surface.

If an illuminated picture of our spiritual and emotional insides could show old fractures, I would also want to understand why certain injuries never saw the fullness of healing. And I have a theory that—at least speaking for myself—the cause would be "She just didn't want to grieve anymore."

Our healing isn't linear. Sometimes we feel a sense of victory and hope in a broken area of our lives, and moments later, we're back on the mat, wondering how we'll ever stand up again. So, this is me asking you in earnest to keep telling God where it hurts.

When a new offense surfaces, when an old one rears its head again after you thought you were finally doing better, don't abandon the act of crying out to the Lord. We don't ever graduate from needing Jesus, and even when we feel "over it," grief will continue to have its way.

REFLECTION QUESTIONS

1. If a scan of your soul was lit up on a medical board, what old wounds might you see?
2. Are there any current injuries you are tired of grieving or paying attention to? Why do you find yourself eager to move on?
3. What could crying out to God look like for you in this season?
4. What's at stake if you ignore the wounds of your past, present, and future?

TODAY'S AFFIRMATION

I am safe to raise my voice with God. I am safe to cry out to Him in the midst of my pain, past and present. I affirm that healing is not linear and that the path to victory may not be as straight or clear as I imagined. But God is with me and for me. He has gone ahead of me and will accommodate my limp and staggered pace. He catches my tears, He comes near to me in compassion, and my sorrow is never too much for Him. I agree that I want to be fully healed. I don't want to leave any old wounds to fester or thwart the abundance of my future.

Lord, I need You, in this and in every season. And I will keep crying out to You with full assurance that You care for me and hear me. Amen.

DAY 17

Let's Go Together

> Carry each other's burdens, and in this way you will fulfill the law of Christ.
>
> Galatians 6:2

I call it Saturday syndrome.

In our family, sleeping in is greatly valued. No one is shamed for it. We love kids who sleep, and we love adults who are well rested. We even plan out our sleeping to accommodate one another. Because, truly, what is better than a night when you don't have to set an alarm?

I never sleep in on Saturdays, though, and that's intentional. This is because the only thing I love more than sleeping in on a Saturday morning is a completely quiet house. As my kids grew older and got on board with a little extended weekend slumber, I realized that I could wake up a little earlier and get *hours* to sip coffee in the stillness while reading, praying, studying, and simply enjoying a clean and quiet house. So now that's what I do on Saturdays. But a few years ago, I learned I have to look out for Saturday syndrome.

Here's how Saturday syndrome presents in my life:

I wake early and enjoy a few serene hours to contemplate life and the Lord, and then I move on to making a plan for the week. I look out over our days, see what is coming our way, and start to make a list of what needs to get done. That awareness of future plans starts to bleed into my plan for *that* particular day, and that's when my pulse starts quickening. I begin feeling an urgency about all that needs to get done and how much is on our plate, and all of a sudden, I am silently screaming in my head, *Why is everyone still asleep? Don't they know we need to cut the grass, go to the grocery store, clean out all our closets, and disinfect the baseboards?*

And by the time my family sleepily stumbles down the stairs, rested and rejuvenated, I am a wild-eyed, frantic woman, the opposite of the peaceful person you want to encounter first thing on a Saturday morning. So much for sleeping in when you wake up to a four-alarm fire, am I right?

I learned to circumvent the chaos I caused on Saturday mornings in several different ways, but one of the most significant shifts I made was this: I stopped trying to do all the family strategizing and planning alone. I realized that we needed to do it *together*.

Saturday morning is great for personal reflection. It is also great for reading because my kids aren't particularly interested in the nerdy theology books I love to read. Saturday morning is even great for meditating because that's not an effective group activity. But when it came to planning, strategizing, and delegating the structure of our lives, that was something I realized we needed to do as a family.

At this point in the healing of your heartbreak, burnout, or brokenness, I am willing to make a prediction that it is time (if you haven't already) to pull others in. There is a point of diminishing returns where we will circle around the same ache, pain, or problem as we stew in solitude. We stop seeing things from other people's perspectives. We stop seeing and hearing other people and the pain they're in. We stop letting ourselves be comforted. We miss out on getting to have our burdens carried by those who currently have a lighter load, and then we stop remembering that we were meant to help carry their burdens as well.

It's so vulnerable to need people. It's so humbling to know that we have hit our own limit of how much we can take care of ourselves. But on the contrary, it's so incredibly wise to turn to the people around us and say, "I need help. I can't do this alone." And some of the healing we're longing for breaks open and begins to rise to the surface when we are brave enough to recognize that we need one another.

Here are the caveats: It may take asking multiple people to find the right safe person. You might realize that, for this particular heartbreak or season of burnout, you need a professional therapist or counselor. You may feel uncomfortable and exposed. Those you reach out to may not help you with perfection or seamless mercy. But you will have taken one huge step toward healing just by asking for help. This is where the light breaks in. This is where we get the help and healing we need.

REFLECTION QUESTIONS

1. In what ways have you been carrying the burden alone?
2. What scares you most about asking for help? What lies does God want to rewrite with His truth when it comes to living in community?

3. How do you feel when others ask you to walk with them?
4. What type of people do you need in this season? What do you most need from them? How can you best ask for that help?

TODAY'S AFFIRMATION

Father, You did not create us to walk alone. I agree, gratefully, that I need others, just as they need me, to walk beside each other from brokenness to breakthrough. I agree that I can be courageous enough to ask for help, and I come into alignment with the mercy and insight that will enable me to serve others around me. Help me to recognize the beauty and strength found in community, where we can fulfill the law of Christ by carrying each other's burdens. I trust in Your grace to guide me as I seek to walk together with others in love and humility. Amen.

DAY 18

Get Back Up Again

We are hard pressed on every side, but not crushed; perplexed, but not in despair; persecuted, but not abandoned; struck down, but not destroyed.

2 Corinthians 4:8–9

I have a fickle relationship with the ocean.

Or maybe it's more of a *humbled* relationship with the ocean.

I honor the sea for what it is, for what God created it to be: wild, vast, majestic, beautiful, and mysterious. Study after study has proven that just being near the ocean has a positive impact on our sense of peace and mental health, but I don't even need the research to know that. I stand on the shore, walk by the water, hear the waves in the background, and I feel the power and presence of God.

But when I start to think about actually getting into the ocean, that's when I get humbled and remember my place.

The first reason I tremble is because I know that the ocean is the shark's house. It's not my house. I don't want the shark to come play in my house, so I think it's pretty preposterous that I go play in his. And it's not *just* the shark's house. It's the jellyfish's playground, the man-of-war's domain, the domicile of the often-underestimated and honestly pretty aggressive dolphin, and that's not even to mention the millions of sea creatures I can't see or name. What's underneath that water is fascinating, but it's none of my business.

If that weren't enough, there are potentially deadly undertows and waves that will make you cry out for your mama. The ocean is seriously beautiful and terrifyingly brutal when it wants to be.

And still, we wade in.

A few months ago, our kids talked us into a family surfing lesson. And as intimidated as I am by the sea, I'll do almost anything for my kids. So I pulled on the wet suit (I also love any family outing that comes with a costume) and sat through the on-land lesson, really feeling like my relationship with the tide might be about to change. I felt competent, cute in my outfit, and as though my core was strong enough to paddle out, jump up, and maybe catch a wave or two.

I wasn't out for ninety seconds before I got whacked in the face with my surfboard. I ran my fingers over my teeth to make sure they were all there. I already have one fake one from an incident with my stainless steel water bottle. My molars all intact, I tried again. And again. And again. My exhaustion was making each attempt harder than the last as my muscles groaned under the weight of each wave. Even as my failure and fatigue weighed me down, I realized that my fear and defeat were slipping away. Because ultimately, this is what we're made to do: get back up again.

As image bearers of God, and as children of the kingdom being renewed, we can access more humility and awe at His power at work in and through us than fear of getting hurt again. We can, by the power that raised Jesus Christ from the dead, look at what is pressing against us on every single side and declare that we will try again once more, in His name and through His strength. As more than conquerors, we can decide that we don't want to live the rest of our lives recounting how badly it hurt to get knocked down. We can partner with God to create a new memory, to tell a new story, one where we courageously grab His hand, stand back up again, and see what will happen as we ride the next wave.

What's wild about coming back from heartbreak, burnout, and brokenness is this: The breakthrough, the healing, the hope are often bound up in the comeback. Many of us wait our whole lives to feel ready to love again, fight again, or try again, but we will wait forever if we wait until there is no longer any possibility of pain. The real victory is in dusting ourselves off without the promise of a painless future, because we are motivated by something more than an easy path.

I don't know what took you out this round.

I can only imagine how terrifying the wave was.

You might still feel the tenderness of the bruises. The feebleness from fresh wounds.

But you are not destroyed.

You are not finished.

This is not the end.

You will get back up again.

In Jesus's name.

REFLECTION QUESTIONS

1. What's your ocean in this season? Are there areas where you feel both awe and fear, where you are drawn in but also humbled by the challenges you face?
2. What was your most recent "wipeout"? How did you respond? What did you learn about God? What did you learn about yourself?
3. What waves have you been hesitant to face again because of past pain or failure? How might God be calling you to step back into those areas with renewed courage and faith?
4. What do you risk missing out on if you don't get back up again? What future freedom, victory, and abundance?

TODAY'S AFFIRMATION

I am a safe, held, and seen child of God, and I can stand firm once again in His promises. I don't have to obey my fear or avoid the waves of life or the challenges that knock me down. Though failure, fatigue, and future pain will be a part of my story, I know that God is with me. He is mighty, and He is good. The foundation of my life is the resilience of Christ. He has not left me or forsaken me. The purpose for my life remains strong, and the power of God in me is not diminished by any defeat, in Jesus's name. This is where I rise again because God is here, and His strength is made perfect in my persistence.

Name It to Claim It (Just Not Like You Think)

You have searched me, LORD,
and you know me.
You know when I sit and when I rise;
you perceive my thoughts from afar.
You discern my going out and my lying down;
you are familiar with all my ways.
Before a word is on my tongue
you, LORD, know it completely.

Psalm 139:1–4

I found out on Mother's Day. At a Walmart, no less.

My husband had sent me to a coffee shop for the afternoon, the height of luxury in a season where money was crazy tight. As my Mother's Day gift, he had encouraged me to go get a big coffee and a treat and to enjoy a few kid-free hours reading, writing, or doing whatever I pleased. I ordered my coffee, and it tasted a little off, but I happily continued my reading and journaling anyway.

Then, on the way home, I stopped by Walmart for some more diapers, and suddenly the sour-tasting coffee made sense. I was in the diaper aisle when I remembered the last time I had turned up my nose at coffee—the *only* time I turned up my nose at coffee—and it was when I was newly pregnant.

So I ran to the pregnancy test aisle, grabbed one, purchased it with the diapers, and took the test in a stall at Walmart. I have never really been a patient person. This would be our fourth, and I smiled from ear to ear that night thinking, *Four. God, You have been so generous to give us what we don't deserve.*

By Father's Day, I'd lost the baby. It started with a heart-breaking and lonely ultrasound, followed by weeks of follow-up appointments, many nights of tears, and a whirlwind of wondering what I had done wrong, feeling wrapped in shame and overwhelming fear. I had barely begun to process the loss, and I was embarrassed about how sad I felt. I thought I should have been more resilient.

During that time, my mom came to me and gently asked why I wasn't allowing myself to grieve. At the time, I wrote a daily blog that hundreds, sometimes thousands, of people read. She asked if I was planning on sharing that we had suffered a loss. She asked a lot of good questions, and all of my sheepish answers were cloaked in shame. I told her how I was worried I was too sad, scared that if I opened the lid on my sadness, I would never be able to get it back in my body. She encouraged me to be honest anyway, to share our story—and not necessarily for anyone else's benefit but first for my own.

And so I did.

We decided to name the baby Arrow. I bought him a blanket, and I bought a new robe, since I had purchased a new robe for the hospital with each new baby that entered our family. I wore this one to grieve, but it was something, a marking that made this life seem real to our home. He had really happened, if ever so quickly, and we were changed by the love and by the loss.

We think that hiding our grief makes it go away, but it is actually naming it that often ushers in our healing. We think minimizing our loss makes us seem strong, but often it leaves us weakened in our wounded places, unable to utilize the victory we would have experienced had we let ourselves feel. We think it's our moments of winning, shining triumph in the light of everyone else's adoration that turns us into champions, but it's often the compassion and mercy we receive in the dark that grow us the most.

When we name our pain, we claim its healing.

When we name our loss, we claim the gain heaven offers us in the midst of it.

When we name our weaknesses, we gain access to His strength.

When we make space for our grief, our questions, and our groaning, we also make space for love, passion, and tenderness.

Naming what you lost is the beginning of your healing.

Naming a season as one of healing is often the beginning of breakthrough.

Naming what you've healed from is the beginning of your ministry.

REFLECTION QUESTIONS

1. What unspoken grief or loss are you carrying that needs to be named out loud before yourself, God, and others?
2. How has hiding your pain weighed you down? What might change if you brought it into the light?
3. What has God's compassion and mercy looked like in the darkest moments of your life?
4. What would it look like to name this season of loss, pain, and healing for what it is?

TODAY'S AFFIRMATION

My Father knows me, sees me, and holds me. He is present in the hidden corners of my heart, in the dark shadows of my story, where grief and pain reside. Before I name my pain, He knows it, but today I choose to name my pain before Him and to affirm my intimacy and nearness to Him. My grief is not a sign of weakness but an invitation to experience His deep compassion and love. I am safe to name my pain and allowed to claim my healing. As I name my loss, I also claim the healing and hope He offers.

Father, I believe that You are turning my mourning into a testimony of Your grace. Thank You for knowing me, loving me, and carrying me through every season. In Jesus's name, Amen.

Rest Along the Way

There remains, then, a Sabbath-rest for the people of God; for anyone who enters God's rest also rests from their works, just as God did from his. Let us, therefore, make every effort to enter that rest, so that no one will perish by following their example of disobedience.

Hebrews 4:9–11

Rest is a beautiful principle, but most of us feel like it's hard to access in moments of pain. How do we rest when it feels like our world is falling apart? How do we disconnect from the noise when a devastating call could come in at any moment? What does a "day off" mean when you can't take a day off from your pain? What happens when you're so burnt out and fatigued that rest doesn't really seem to work anymore?

Where is the rest for those in the thick of heartbreak, burnout, and brokenness?

Prior to the year our lives seemed to come apart, my husband and I had a pretty well-developed rest and Sabbath routine. We taught other people how to rest. I had written a book on realistic rest. We weren't experts by any means, but we knew how to take a much-needed deep breath.

And then, suddenly, in a season where we were desperate for respite, there was little to no release available. Our problems followed us into the moments we weren't working; family crises meant there were always more calls to make, and we both felt utterly behind because trauma and grief were seeping into our working hours. The rhythms we had established flew out the window, and even when we tried to engage in our regular routines, they weren't as life-giving or refreshing as they had once been.

But I'm grateful that some principles and truths stood firm in our hearts and souls. Some characteristics of kingdom rest acted like buoys in a stormy sea. We gasped and grasped until we reached them, grabbed hold, and experienced some moments of reprieve.

The most anchoring truth for us in the middle of heartbreak was the good news that heaven is coming.

Real rest and full recovery aren't wholly available to us on earth. We're not off base when we feel like life is trying to take us out. Living in a fallen world is just too much sometimes. Living in a fallen world often feels like we are getting tossed and swamped and swallowed whole by the waves around us. But heaven is the promise that, one day, the striving will cease and we will finally breathe. Our cultivation and community in heaven won't be stressful or taxing. We won't be moving from one crisis to the next; we will know peace. We will know true rest.

This might not sound like good news right now, as it involves waiting for our future hope, but this deep knowledge can settle and soothe us: It's not supposed to be this way, and it won't always be this way.

Another principle about kingdom rest served my husband and me well when everything was wild around us. We remembered that there are different kinds of rest, and when we couldn't access one, we could lean into another.

Because there are multiple types of fatigue, there are also various ways to experience rest. Our family focused on the four main types: spiritual, physical, emotional, and mental. In the midst of heartbreak and grief, emotional rest was hard to come by. With heavy hearts, we couldn't just name our feelings and put them on a shelf. But we could intentionally choose physical, spiritual, and mental rest through strategies like getting enough sleep, asking others to pray for us at our lowest moments, and premaking decisions so we weren't overwhelmed by decision fatigue.

On the flip side, in seasons when I felt physically exhausted, seeing no relief in sight (like having a newborn or caring for a sick parent in the hospital), I couldn't snap my fingers and have more physical energy, but I could rest in the other areas, such as recovering some margin spiritually, mentally, and emotionally.

There is nothing restful about someone criticizing you in the midst of an already hard season about how you need to do better at making rest a priority. So I won't do that. Instead, I will simply remind you of the words that have helped me hold on when the storm threatens to sweep me away:

It's not always going to be this way.

Real rest is coming.

You don't have to hold it all together.

God is good at His job.

Rest where you can, when you can, because it's God's gift to you—not something He wants from you.

Amen?

REFLECTION QUESTIONS

1. What is exhausting you right now? Does it feel physically, mentally, emotionally, or spiritually heavy?
2. What are the truths that have served as buoys for you in this storm? How can you continue to cling to them?
3. How can you shift your perspective of rest from something you have to "get better" at toward viewing it as a gift from God meant to sustain you? How can you practically rest in this season?
4. What's at risk if you don't rest? What will happen if you don't receive the relief God is offering you?

TODAY'S AFFIRMATION

I won't let the chaos of life steal the good gift of rest that God has promised me. I break ties with the all-consuming pressure to hold it all together. My strength is in God, not in my own striving to keep my head above water. The relentless storms and burdens of this world will surround me but not overtake me because I know that real rest is coming. I choose to rest when and where I can, trusting that God's peace will sustain me through every trial. I affirm that I am not alone in my struggles; God is good at His job, and He is faithful to provide the rest I need in every season. As I wait for the fullness of His rest in heaven, I will embrace His gift of rest now, in whatever form it comes, knowing that it is a reflection of His love and grace. Amen.

It's Time to Stop Coping

God is our refuge and strength,
an ever-present help in trouble.
Psalm 46:1

I feel like coping mechanisms get a bad reputation.

We make them out to be villains when really they're often tools—buoys to help us float when we might otherwise drown.

In the weeks that followed my stepdad's funeral, I tried to get back into the groove of life, but I just wasn't quite ready. None of us were. We had jobs, children, and churches to lead. There was, of course, a beautiful grace period extended to us by our beloved community. But while time and space were given to us to grieve, when you're utterly heartbroken and traumatized, it feels like there's never enough time to truly heal.

Around that time, I went to coffee with my mentor, and I decided to be uncomfortably honest about a few coping mechanisms I was using to get through the day. I wasn't harming myself—I wasn't doing anything illegal—but I was skipping the healthy rhythms that made me feel whole during easier seasons. I was watching TV more than I was reading my Bible. I was eating basically any sugar or carb that came my way. I was staying up much later than normal because sleep made me feel sad or panicked. I was coping.

I asked my mentor if she thought those behaviors were okay or if they were things I needed to cut out immediately or figure out how to quit. She looked pensive for a moment and then gently said, "Not this week. Maybe not even this month. But keep asking me, and I'll be honest with you."

Coping mechanisms are the strategies we often use to help us endure the stress and trauma of life. A therapist I once knew told me, "There's nothing wrong with trying to help yourself feel better." And while many of us might balk at that idea, it's true. Wanting to feel better, to heal and be out of pain, is not selfish or hedonistic—it's human.

I've kept that phrase in my head for the past few years, using it as a compassionate guide when I see myself or others reaching for a coping mechanism. But in the time since I first heard it, I have added my own words to the end of the sentence.

"There's nothing wrong with trying to help yourself feel better *unless what you're reaching for won't actually help*."

Once you learn that a coping mechanism isn't serving you, and once you're ready to face whatever it is you have been trying to distract yourself from, it's time to open up your hands. It's time to drop what you've been carrying and embrace the abundance God has purchased for you.

Because we were meant for so much more than coping.

We were meant for more than just getting by.

We don't have to stay stuck in patterns of trying to help ourselves feel better when we have access to the God of the universe, who has promised to be our ever-present help in times of trouble.

And there is a wild victory in dusting ourselves off, putting down those coping mechanisms, and running to the source of life and light, of healing and wholeness, so we can finally walk in freedom.

I don't know exactly where you are in this season of heartbreak, burnout, or brokenness. I don't know what your coping mechanisms are, if you feel convicted or concerned about them, or if you will need to pull in some outside help to put them down. But I do know that Jesus is better than anything else. I do know that He is near to the brokenhearted, that He is the most resilient refuge and the most secure strength. I know that He won't leave us wondering, wandering, or feeling like we might have wasted our time.

I know that, in His presence, we won't feel distracted from our pain or distanced from our troubles. We will experience His power and presence in a profound way that will leave us able to do much more than just endure. He won't leave us to merely cope, He will lead us to hope.

Your story isn't about just getting by. It's time to stand in victory.

REFLECTION QUESTIONS

1. On a scale of 1–10, how concerned are you about your current coping mechanisms?
2. Take a moment to identify what those coping strategies are. How might they be offering you temporary relief while ultimately leaving you feeling stuck?

3. What would surrender look like in regard to your coping mechanisms?
4. Can you honestly affirm, even in the midst of your struggle, that God's presence is more powerful than any coping mechanism you have been holding on to? There are no wrong answers.

TODAY'S AFFIRMATION

I am a beloved child of God, and I trust in His unfailing strength and refuge. There is therefore now no condemnation for those who are in Christ Jesus, and my shame was purchased on the cross of Christ. I don't have to rely on temporary fixes or fleeting comforts to get through my days. Though I may be walking through seasons of heartbreak, burnout, or brokenness, I know that God is my ever-present help in times of trouble. My life is built on His love, and His purpose remains unshaken by my fatigue or fear. In Jesus's name, I declare that I was made for more than coping. I was made to thrive. This is where victory begins because God is with me, and His presence is more powerful than any coping mechanism I could ever reach for.

DAY 22

Let's Enter Back In

I waited patiently for the LORD;
he inclined to me and heard my cry.
He drew me up from the pit of destruction,
out of the miry bog,
and set my feet upon a rock,
making my steps secure.
He put a new song in my mouth,
a song of praise to our God.

Psalm 40:1–3 ESV

It was an unintentional but necessary break.

The last time I had preached on a Sunday at our church was Palm Sunday, the Sunday before Easter, the Sunday before the week that changed everything for our family.

My stepdad, one of my biggest encouragers and champions, the one we called "the mayor of Bright City," sat on the third row that Palm Sunday, in his usual spot, beaming and shouting "amen" along the way. He told me afterward that it was his favorite message he had heard me preach, and I received that encouragement the way I usually did: grateful and sure I would hear it from him again.

But, unexpectedly, he passed away. And while I didn't mean to take such a long break from preaching, it just happened—and it needed to.

My grief was thick, my faith was rocked, and the heartaches kept coming, wave after wave. Before I knew it, I was in a pit. I had crawled my way out of similar pits before, so I knew I wouldn't remain in this one forever. But I also knew there would be no standing before the church, microphone in hand, feeling competent and ready to share the gospel anytime soon. Not just yet.

The thing about pits is this: Sometimes you immediately want to get out. And sometimes it seems wise to just go ahead and get cozy down there. Maybe you could have someone throw a couch down. Maybe it's nicer and quieter down in the pit. Maybe it feels safer to be in a place where no one can get to you. Maybe the pit you have feared your entire life, the one you would never have chosen, suddenly seems easier than the outside world. Maybe emerging into the harsh light is scarier than staying stuck.

My break from preaching was unintentional. And I think we all have things—callings, dreams, desires, giftings, roles, rhythms, and responsibilities—that we need to get back to when the time is right. Sometimes it just takes time for us to get back on that horse, to enter back into our callings, and sometimes it takes a tug from the Lord or from our communities, or even just a swift soul-kick in the form of a devotional.

But do you know what is needed for all of us, more than anything? A reminder that our God, our good Father, is the pit-rescuer.

He was down there with us all along, whether we fell in or dug the ditch ourselves.

He is good, caring, compassionate, and ever present, whether we can't wait to get out of our pit or we have started thinking of it as home.

And He will lift us out, cradle our heads, and secure our feet in the name of Jesus. By grace, through faith, He will put a new song in our mouths.

I preached again for the first time a few months later, and I was shakier and more tender than I could have anticipated. My stepdad wasn't there, but my Father was.

I didn't sound the way I used to. My faith now has a beautiful limp, and my voice trembles. I would rather not have either, but I am grateful to be standing at all.

I have a new song, richer and born of more knowledge because of the gift of suffering. I have a new victory that wasn't earned through winning but through losing. I have a wild hope that is anchored in heaven. I have eyes that can sustain a gaze on the broken things of this world because I'm more sure than ever it won't always be this way.

I waited (sometimes not so patiently) for the Lord, and He always heard my cry.

At times, I didn't even want Him to come because I was scared of what it might mean, of what might happen when the crying stopped, who I would be and what I would find to be true of Him.

He drew me up from the pit of destruction with eternal kindness and compassion in His eyes.

He took me out of the dangerous fog, the haze that threatened to overtake me, and set my feet upon a rock, making my steps secure.

He put a new song in my mouth, a renewed and sustained song of praise to our God.

And He will do it again and again.

REFLECTION QUESTIONS

1. What pit are you in right now? How do you feel about it? How do you think God feels about it?
2. How has your faith shifted in this season? What feels stronger or more fragile? What would it look like to embrace the security of faith and the sacred tremble of courage as you move forward?
3. Think about the callings, dreams, rhythms, or roles that you have pressed pause on in the midst of heaviness. Are you scared to step back in? Have you asked God if the time is right?
4. What new song has He given you to sing? How has it shifted from the old words that worked before?

TODAY'S AFFIRMATION

I am a cherished child of God, and He is always moving toward me with compassion, ready to rescue me. He is my Rock and my Refuge, and no pit is too deep and no darkness too overwhelming for Him to find me and lift me up. The pit may be comfortable, but I was made for more than hiding. It won't be my striving, pretending, or strategy that gets me out. It will be His voice and His hand, His calling and His strength. My grief, fears, and hesitations do not define me, nor do they hold the final word in my life. I declare that my steps are secure, not because my future path will be painless but because I cannot shake the presence or power of God. My Father is with me and for me. This is where healing begins, where songs are sung. Victory is my future.

DAY 23

Remember Those Who Stood with You

> Greet Priscilla and Aquila, my co-workers in Christ Jesus. They risked their lives for me. Not only I but all the churches of the Gentiles are grateful to them.
>
> Romans 16:3–4

I'm horrible at thank-you notes.

My mom is the kind of woman who hands you a thank-you note before the wrapping paper from the gift has been thrown away. She is *incredible* at thank-you notes.

It's not that I'm not thankful. I just lack the follow-through to write the note. And on the rare occasion that I *do* write one, it finds a new home in the abyss of whatever current purse I am carrying, rarely making it out of my hands and into theirs.

When I clean out my room or closet a few times a year, I find twelve thank-you notes and then have to decide if it is even worth attempting a second delivery. I will confess that I have often resorted to just taking a picture of the note that never made it and texting it to the person I originally intended to thank.

But you know who wasn't bad at thank-you notes? The apostle Paul.

I recently found out that many theologians believe that, on the few occasions Paul wasn't overly expressive of his gratitude at the beginning of a letter, it was on purpose. It was meant to set a tone.

We know from meeting Priscilla and Aquila in several New Testament texts that they were good friends with Paul. In Acts 18, we see how they showed him hospitality and also became his ministry partners, offering their house as a place for the church in Ephesus to gather. They helped disciple Apollos, the eloquent teacher many believed would go on to author the book of Hebrews and who was a catalytic figure in the development of the early church. And then, of course, Paul just says it outright in his letter to the Romans: Priscilla and Aquila risked their lives for him. They stuck out their necks for Paul.

We don't know all the things Priscilla and Aquila did to make Paul so thankful for them.

What we do know is this: The apostle Paul ministered to thousands during his lifetime. He traveled to them and for them. He wrote letter upon letter, many of which became canonical Scripture. He shared the gospel with individuals, ministered to churches, pioneered communities, witnessed in jails, was shipwrecked, battled illness, and essentially had his life wrung out for the glory of God and for the early church.

He ministered to thousands and only thanked a very small fraction of those people.

And I wonder if he ever felt like he was doing so much for everyone else without knowing who stood by *him*. I wonder if he ever felt alone, risking his life and cultural standing for the sake of a gospel that made many think he was crazy.

I don't know exactly how Paul felt in his hardship, when he was heartbroken, burnt out, and burdened. But I do know how I feel—incredibly lonely.

Because who else knows the exact pain that I have endured besides Jesus?

Who else knows how hard it is for me to press through and show up when I don't want to?

Who else knows how hard endurance was on those bleak nights?

Who else saw me crying and stayed?

My kind Friend and Savior, Jesus. He was there. He is there for you too.

The truth is, there were a few other people there for me too.

I texted my friends Anna, Alex, and Amanda on the darkest day of my grief.

And there was Kristen. I showed up at her house with wild eyes, with the shock of pain spreading across my face. My husband dropped everything when I texted, "Come back to the hospital. We need you." My team at work had pictures printed for the funeral, then had them framed so I didn't have to comb through a thousand beautiful, painful memories.

And so many others were there.

Of course, there were moments when I felt lonely.

But God never left me totally alone.

Out of all the people I'd call my friends, and in the thousands of people I "know"—either online or through various communities—not all could be there. They didn't all get it.

But there were a few who did.

And while none of them showed up perfectly, I don't want to let the haze of grief and pain cause me to forget to thank them now that the fog has cleared.

We have to remember those who stood with us on our darkest days. They are God's kindness to us. It's important that we remember their names so we *can* thank them, but also so we can be empowered to show up for others on their darkest days. So we can use the comfort we have so richly received to comfort others. And maybe, for those of us who are having a hard time identifying even just a few people, we will be more inspired to stand with others in the future.

I pray that a few names are coming to you now, but if you can't name even one or two, you can name Jesus. He is enough. He sustains. He holds us. He carries us. Even when we forget His presence.

Now, if you will excuse me, I have some thank-you notes to write.

REFLECTION QUESTIONS

1. Who was there for you in your grief? What did they do? What did they say? How can you thank them?
2. What did God do for you on the dark days when no one else was there? Have you thanked Him?
3. Have you ever refused to show up for someone God called you to comfort in their crisis? There is no condemnation, but use this time to confess.
4. How do you want to show up for others in the future?

TODAY'S AFFIRMATION

I wasn't purchased into the kingdom of God as an orphan. I was purchased into a family. I want to acknowledge and show gratitude for those who have shown up, risked their own comfort, and offered their friendship to me when I felt most desperate. They have been the body of Christ for me, the hands of comfort and the mouth of wisdom. In Jesus's name, I commit to honoring them. And I commit to honoring God's kindness to me by standing with others on their darkest days. My gratitude will take root and grow beautiful fruit because my Father is able to make beauty from ashes.

Notice Your Muscles

For this reason, since the day we heard about you, we have not stopped praying for you. We continually ask God to fill you with the knowledge of his will through all the wisdom and understanding that the Spirit gives, so that you may live a life worthy of the Lord and please him in every way: bearing fruit in every good work, growing in the knowledge of God, being strengthened with all power according to his glorious might so that you may have great endurance and patience, and giving joyful thanks to the Father, who has qualified you to share in the inheritance of his holy people in the kingdom of light.

Colossians 1:9–12

They call them NSVs.

Non-scale victories.

I have done a good amount of ministry in the area of body image, mainly because I have lived so many years in bondage to body shame. When God set me free, I couldn't keep quiet about what I'd learned. When you want to shift people away from being obsessed with a number on the scale and encourage general health and wellness instead, you need an NSV.

A non-scale victory is any functional piece of fruit in the fight for physical health: Maybe you have more energy to chase your kids on the playground, or you start sleeping through the night, or you have enough energy to make it through a day of vacation without taking a nap. NSVs are one way to break ties with a culture of striving for an arbitrary goal—like a certain number on the scale—and instead help us refocus our desires on overall growth.

I have one NSV, one benchmark at the top of my health goals for the foreseeable future: I want to be able to lift heavier weights than my son Benjamin. He is already faster than me—that ship has sailed—he was taller than me before he turned fourteen. And right now, at the time I write this, he has me beat on the bench press and pull-ups, but I can still school him on almost any other major weight-lifting effort. My efforts are probably futile—he loves working out and is just getting started—but it's nice to try to keep up, you know?

A few months ago, Benja (our nickname for him) gave me the best compliment anyone has ever given me. Unprompted, he remarked that my triceps looked very defined. I don't think he said it that clearly or even that nicely, but he definitely pointed it out. Like any middle-aged mom who is desperate for her teenage son to think she is cool, I pretended like I barely heard him and then immediately marked the day in my journal.

Who cares how much you weigh or what size pants you wear if your teenage son is impressed by your triceps?

I have this hunch that you and I would never have chosen the hardship we are currently experiencing. We would have bypassed the heartbreak, burnout, and brokenness if we could have. We would have happily kept living without a need for healing or breakthrough, and yet, here we are. Burnt out. Broken. Needy.

And part of our healing, our victory, and the process of breakthrough is believing that God has used this situation to shape us for the better, looking for the new muscles He has grown in us. We don't have to wait for others to come alongside us and point out the proof. We can use our spiritual eyes to examine our own souls and speak life where we see it.

Right here, in the most broken and barren places, God has brought new life.

It's time for you to notice your new muscles.

What has shifted in your endurance?

How has He grown your patience?

Has your worship or prayer life matured?

How are your levels of compassion?

What have you learned about unshakable joy?

Have your affections for God been stirred?

Do you have fresh insight into the peace that surpasses understanding?

Are you eager to comfort others with the comfort you yourself have received?

You don't need anyone to come along and call out the fruit.

You know where God has grown you the most, and you're going to give that glory back to Him.

REFLECTION QUESTIONS

1. What are your new muscles? Thank God for them.
2. Take it a step further: How do you know a breakthrough is near?

3. What are you learning about God in this season that you didn't know before? What are you learning about yourself that you didn't know before?
4. Are there any new muscles in those around you that you could notice and affirm to encourage them?

TODAY'S AFFIRMATION

I am not scared to celebrate the victory God has worked within me, through me, and around me. I see the growth and thank Him for the strength He has developed in my heart, even if no one else notices it. I may not have chosen this season, but I trust that God has used it to cultivate in me endurance, patience, and a deeper love for Him. In Jesus's name, I declare that I am stronger now and still growing—not because of my own might but because He is the bringer of new life and fresh fruit. When I see new muscles develop, all the glory goes to Him. Things are growing. Things are changing. Breakthrough has arrived.

DAY 25

Celebrate Anyway

> Those who sow with tears
>   will reap with songs of joy.
> Those who go out weeping,
>   carrying seed to sow,
> will return with songs of joy,
>   carrying sheaves with them.
>
> Psalm 126:5–6

Welcome to my birthday soapbox.

Wherever you land on this divisive issue, you are welcome here.

I love to celebrate my birthday.

Notice the intention of my words; I'm not saying that I love it when *other people* celebrate my birthday. I'm grateful if they're there! I'm thankful for the community! I need other people to dance with and help eat the cake. I can't do that all on my own. But I am not putting pressure on other people to make me feel celebrated because I know exactly how I want to mark the occasion and have likely been planning it for months prior to the celebration.

I think somewhere along the way, people who enjoy celebrating their birthdays got falsely labeled as self-centered or egotistical. And maybe some people fall into both categories. But some of us are just trying to stop and honor each passing year and the things God has done to bring us to yet another birthday. Some of us just need a day to proclaim how grateful we are. And that's me.

Now, conversely, I have a hard time relating to people who don't enjoy their birthdays. My assumption is that, if you don't want to celebrate, you've had some trauma in this area. Maybe it was serious trauma that happened on your special day, or maybe someone slighted you at your party, or maybe someone significant to you made it seem like enjoying your birthday was selfish, so you felt like you weren't allowed to. I know that many of us might not have been raised in families that let us take up space, and so we might not have been encouraged to honor significant or special days. So, while I might not relate to you, I can understand how you got there.

Because of my proclivity toward celebrating, I usually plan my own parties. Sometimes it's an actual party, and sometimes I just design a day that sounds life-giving and then invite my family or close friends. If I do have some sort of gathering, I like to decide the details. I have been known to buy my guests gifts or even design something for them. One year, it was wine glasses with a verse I wanted them to pray for me, and another year, it was individualized friendship bracelets with personalized colors to show them how they make me feel. But this past year, I didn't have it in me.

The grief was too loud.

There was so much brokenness in our life that it didn't look the way it was supposed to look.

And I was too tired, too exhausted, to plan anything.

And so, my husband and friends did the most gracious thing they could do and kicked me out of the planning. I was so grateful despite being a little uncomfortable at not being in charge of the strategizing.

A week or two out from the big day, I found myself crying to my husband, profusely expressing my thanks for all he had planned but confessing that I just didn't have it in me. There was too much sadness in my heart to celebrate.

I'm grateful that he politely declined my request to cancel everything.

And he told me a slightly more eloquent version of what I'm about to tell you.

We must continue to celebrate in the midst of our heartbreak, burnout, and brokenness. We celebrate because, even when things seem bleak, another year, another day, and even another hour is a holy and significant thing and worth thanking God for. We celebrate in the midst of our heartbreak, burnout, and brokenness not to convince ourselves that things aren't hard but to prophetically declare that we won't be crying forever (see Rev. 21:4).

> Those who sow with tears
>   will reap with songs of joy.
> Those who go out weeping,
>   carrying seed to sow,
> will return with songs of joy,
>   carrying sheaves with them. (Ps. 126:5–6)

Our sorrow will be replaced with joy, and our weeping will one day become rejoicing.

Maybe not today or tomorrow.

Maybe not as quickly as we'd hope.

Maybe, probably, not even fully while we're here on earth.

But we celebrate, even in the midst of brokenness, to remind our souls that one day we will celebrate forever in a place where there is no brokenness to be seen. And we celebrate in the midst of brokenness because we are unwilling to wait until heaven to worship God for all He has done.

You don't have to pretend that it's all fine.

You can celebrate with a limp.

You can cry when the party is over, or maybe even during it, as you express your gratitude to God for getting you through this season.

You can be alone with a journal or call in the cavalry to help you blow out the literal or metaphorical candles.

But you can't wait to celebrate.

Celebrating right now? This is what victory looks like.

REFLECTION QUESTIONS

1. What is your typical approach to celebration? What would celebrating look like in this season?
2. How does Psalm 126 make you feel? What does it stir up in you?
3. In what ways can you intentionally honor the growth you have experienced over the past year despite the challenges you have faced?
4. What would it look like to invite others in to celebrate with you or even to help you celebrate in the midst of your own trials or pain right now?

TODAY'S AFFIRMATION

I refuse to let the weight of brokenness and fatigue silence my celebration. I will not be held captive by the brokenness around me because, even in the midst of pain, I can thank God. I choose to rejoice today, not because joy comes easily but because I want to declare that real restoration and healing are coming. My tears today will sow seeds of joy tomorrow, and I trust that God will turn my sorrow into pure celebration at the right time. I will not wait for the pain to subside before I praise Him; instead, I thank God that I can hold space for both weeping and rejoicing. Every day, every year, every moment is a gift from God, and I will honor Him by celebrating right now.

Sleep Like It's Solved

> You rise up early, and go to bed late, and work hard for your food, all for nothing. For the Lord gives to His loved ones even while they sleep.
>
> Psalm 127:2 NLV

I'm already not a great sleeper.

I come from a long line of women who adapted to living with less sleep so they could take care of people, problems, ministry, and family when they needed to. And sometimes we "needed" to be awake, not so we could take care of anyone or anything physically but so our minds could work out a problem.

The downside of neuroplasticity, the brain's ability to change and grow, is that it can change and grow in negative ways. For example, if you are feeling anxious or concerned about any kind of hardship or heaviness in your life and you stay awake worrying about it, and that problem gets better or simply doesn't grow any worse, the next morning your brain will conclude that staying awake works.

This is how my adult-onset fear of flying was explained to me: It took just one bumpy flight that landed safely *after* I panicked for my brain to learn that anxiety "worked" in keeping my body safe. It's not necessarily logical because it's not conscious, but our brains grow and create new processes and patterns this way, so it's up to us to slow our thoughts down and evaluate whether or not we want them to turn into beliefs.

Because of this inherited condition, this proclivity to stay awake through the most normal seasons, I am often extra anxious when I encounter heartbreak or brokenness in my life, knowing how much it could impact my sleep. In the middle of a stressful meeting that I know will haunt me later on, my mind wanders from the present and flashes an image of me in the middle of the night, still worrying about how the meeting went. Of course, then I am pulled away from actually doing anything productive in that moment. I pre-grieve the sleep I won't get.

Once, a few months ago, I sat with one of my kids in the middle of a heartbreaking conversation. I wanted my face to look compassionate, and I wanted my words to convey kindness and mercy, but all I could think was, *Lord, how will I ever go to sleep tonight after hearing this?*

Another memory: We were standing in the fluorescent-lit hallway after stopping by the hospital one more time for the night as a family. The nurse pulled me aside and said, "Leave your phone number on the board in case I can't reach your mom." I promised her I would turn the volume up so I could hear it ring in my sleep, but in my mind, I knew there was no way I would be getting any sleep that night.

But here's the amazing thing about neuroplasticity: Our brain can learn new pathways. So, in the same way it can learn that middle-of-the-night worry "works," it can also be taught something new and holy.

I recently began using breath prayers as a way to reroute my thoughts when my brain and body reject sleep in the midst of heartache.

A breath prayer is a short, potentially repetitive phrase you say in coordination with inhaling and exhaling. Aligning the prayer with our breathing aids us in using different parts of our brain to calm our nervous system, regulate anxiety and worry, and create new memories and thought patterns that can become the very truths we rely on.

Here are some of my favorites:

(*Inhale*) You keep him in perfect peace
(*Exhale*) whose mind is stayed on you. (Isa. 26:3 ESV)

(*Inhale*) I release everyone and everything
(*Exhale*) to You, my good, good Father.

(*Inhale*) I am not God.
(*Exhale*) He is good at His job.

And, finally . . .

(*Inhale*) I can and will sleep
(*Exhale*) like this problem will be solved.

Sometimes, the breath prayers work like a sleeping pill. Other times, I wrestle for a few hours, prying open the hands of my heart as I surrender to Him. Sometimes, in my folly, I mentally take the problem back and try to fix it, until I remember that He is kind and good, powerful and present, near and omniscient. Over time, I have learned that true victory is the ability to sleep in the midst of crises, the way Jesus did on the boat in the midst of a storm, because even if a particular problem persists, healing is ultimately on the way.

REFLECTION QUESTIONS

1. How has worry or anxiety affected your rest? What core beliefs are at the heart of that struggle?
2. What new core beliefs do you want your brain to learn in this season? Are there particular breath prayers or verses that come to mind that reinforce these truths?
3. What has God done for you in the past, even when you thought you were the one in control? Can you rehearse some of those testimonies to encourage yourself now?
4. If you can sleep at night like God is on His throne, what would it look like for you to rest in God's power and provision during the daytime?

TODAY'S AFFIRMATION

I am not responsible for fixing every problem, holding the world together, calming every storm, healing every affliction, or even providing my own peace. My identity is that of a much-loved child. My Father won't leave or forsake me, and abandoning me in the midst of pain is not part of His character. He has never asked me to stay awake to solve any crisis. He has never asked me to stay awake and do His job. In the name of Jesus, by the power that helped Him rest on the sea in the midst of the storm, I agree with the truth that I can sleep like it's solved. Even if it won't ever be on this side of heaven.

DAY 27

Get Generous

> We want you to know, brothers [and sisters], about the grace of God that has been given among the churches of Macedonia, for in a severe test of affliction, their abundance of joy and their extreme poverty have overflowed in a wealth of generosity on their part. For they gave according to their means, as I can testify, and beyond their means, of their own accord, begging us earnestly for the favor of taking part in the relief of the saints—and this, not as we expected, but they gave themselves first to the Lord and then by the will of God to us.
>
> 2 Corinthians 8:1–5 ESV

Sometimes it feels like nuance is over. Like we've forgotten how to do it as a society. We ride on a heavy pendulum that swings from one perspective to the other. The problem is that this wrecking ball of broad strokes often carries us further from a kingdom perspective, further from compassion and community, and further from victory in Christ.

I see this lack of nuance present in the self-care-versus-selfishness debate. We need to ditch the black-and-white, good-or-bad debate and embrace a more colorful conversation for the sake of our souls.

The phrase *self-care* was coined in the 1950s, when the medical community used it to describe practices that would help patients regain self-worth after traumatic events. It has been used more frequently since the attacks on September 11, when the media and cultural leaders began having more conversations regarding individual recovery after crisis, and the term was mainstreamed in the media by 2016.

It was only shortly after that when I heard Christians begin denouncing the idea as selfish. I remember once, at a women's conference, I heard an entire anti-self-care message that was based on Jesus living a life in which He cared for others and gave up His rights for those He came to serve.

The problem with a message like this is that it is missing nuance. Yes, Jesus was the most selfless human ever to live. Yes, He gave up heaven to come to earth, where He gave up His life by spending His days healing, teaching, loving, and giving. He also practiced some self-care.

He frequently withdrew from crowds to be with His Father or to rest. He ate when He was hungry. He slept when He was tired. He corrected those who tried to stop people from ministering to Him. He drew boundaries. He held boundaries. He kept His inner circle small. And He even begged for any other way, other than the cross, in the garden of Gethsemane.

He wasn't selfish when practicing self-care; He was showing us that generosity and the wisdom of self-care are not at war with one another. Not only are these concepts not mutually exclusive, they actually work best in tandem. Together, they acknowledge the complexity of who we are: sinner-saints formed from dust but also created in the image of God.

And this is what I am reminded of when Paul begins by encouraging the Corinthians with the example of the generous Macedonians: When it looks like you have nothing to give, nothing to offer, and when everyone else tells you this is your season to receive instead of give, God often has something else in mind.

In the kingdom, we don't have to choose between being takers and being givers. We get to be both in almost every season. I have lived through horrific days, as I know you have, where I was convinced I had nothing left to give. I have endured seasons when I had to draw boundaries in order to heal rather than continually pour out from what felt like a broken and barren heart. But almost always, the path back to caring for others comes easier than I imagined because generosity is a part of the path to victory.

I hope that people have cared for you in your season of brokenness, burnout, or heartbreak. I hope you have felt the mercy and nearness of God through His people. I mourn for those of us who have had to receive His care supernaturally because maybe there haven't been compassionate people in our midst. But I know that our healing isn't bound up in us being the only ones to experience generosity, because giving is what we *get* to do, not what we have to do.

Maybe it won't look like it used to. Maybe we will be loving others through prayer where before we gave our time. Maybe we will give words of affirmation or money or hugs. Maybe we will minister in the same ways we always did, but we will carry a new authority because of the afflictions of our past. Maybe we will find an entirely new group of people to be generous with because our Father has been generous with us.

However it looks, we can follow the lead of our Friend and Savior, Jesus, who showed generosity in the midst of His affliction. We can love like Him by wisely setting boundaries and borders in order to better obey God and love His people well.

REFLECTION QUESTIONS

1. Do you see self-care and generosity as being at odds in your life? Are there times when you've favored one over the other to your own detriment?
2. In past seasons, when you've felt like you had nothing left to give, how has God shown you otherwise?
3. In what ways might God be inviting you to redefine generosity in this season? How can you give to others while still honoring your authority to take care of your own body, soul, and mind?
4. How can you mirror Jesus in the way He modeled both kingdom generosity and caring for Himself in this season of your life?

TODAY'S AFFIRMATION

I reject the lie that to take care of myself is selfish, when I know it can be done in humility and alignment with God's Word and will. I will not let the pendulum of extremes pull me away from the kingdom-balanced life that Jesus modeled, a life of generosity and radical self-giving and of receiving rest and renewal as finite creatures. I affirm that generosity is not only a calling but also a gift that brings healing and victory, even in seasons of affliction. I choose to embrace both self-care and selflessness, trusting that in doing so, I will be following the path that leads to true wholeness. I will give of myself where I can, knowing that God honors my boundaries and blesses my efforts. Just as Jesus withdrew to be with the Father, I will prioritize time for rest knowing that, in those moments, I am being equipped to serve others more fully. Amen.

DAY 28

Pray for Breakthrough

Along about midnight, Paul and Silas were at prayer and singing a robust hymn to God. The other prisoners couldn't believe their ears. Then, without warning, a huge earthquake! The jailhouse tottered, every door flew open, all the prisoners were loose.

Acts 16:25–26 MSG

We know what it means to break down, but what does it mean to break through?

Spiritual breakthrough happens when a person, empowered by the Holy Spirit, experiences a profound and transformative shift. Maybe we bypass significant barriers, gain deeper wisdom, or experience a new level of spiritual growth and intimacy with God. Breakthrough makes us see things differently, and when our perspectives shift, our behaviors and rhythms often change too. We think differently about God and His kingdom, so we live differently, and we feel differently.

But what's wild and beautiful about breakthroughs is that, often, nothing needs to change in our circumstances for *us* to change. God is so kind to give us everything we need for transformation right here in our valleys of pain or our mountains of grief.

And I pray that as you've read this book, you have experienced little sips of breakthrough as your mind has been renewed by His Word and your spirit has made new agreements with His power and truth. I hope that some of the factors that led you to initially ask what comes next have begun to shift. But in case they haven't, I do trust that God—our good Father, our Friend Jesus, and the wild Spirit that hovered over the waters at creation—has changed you, in the same way He has been graciously changing me.

My proclivity is to settle into surrender so deeply that I just accept the circumstances as they are, and I stop asking God to do what only He can do: to shake the walls and to supernaturally tear down the bars that have led to my pain and brokenness.

We have looked at so many moments in the apostle Paul's life where he chased after breakthrough in the midst of his own circumstances. He chose gratitude, he spoke life, he remembered those who stood with him, and he grieved and declared his contentment in the midst of ridiculous hardship.

But sometimes God just has to send an earthquake to set us free from our pain. Sometimes the Spirit just has to blow and shift hearts. Sometimes the supernatural breakthrough isn't internal—it's not our heart changing from reflection—it is instead the rush of a miracle that no one saw coming.

In Acts 16, we see Paul seemingly ready to receive a miraculous moment because of the internal work that God has done.

He is not shocked by God's power in providing rescue for him out of nowhere. He doesn't need time to prove it, to process it, to communicate the path of his behaviors that provoked God to be good. He receives the miracle and even stewards it by going on to comfort the frightened jailers, leading them to Jesus and utilizing the favor that would come from others seeing God's faithfulness in his life.

What if our internal moments of breakthrough aren't just strengthening us to endure the heartbreak, burnout, and brokenness of this season? What if God isn't just helping us to get through it? What if He wants us to keep asking for the unimaginable miracle? What if He wants us to keep craving physical healing in our lives and in the lives of the people we love?

What if we start praying for the walls to shake?

What if we let ourselves hope?

What if we prepare for supernatural provision?

What if we ask God to help us take hold of a miracle?

What if we ask Him to change not only our hearts but the hearts of other people in our life?

What if we stop waiting for the other shoe to drop and start waiting for the blessing to fall?

What if we pray for a breakthrough, in Jesus's name?

REFLECTION QUESTIONS

1. What are the internal breakthroughs you have experienced in this season? How have they changed your perspective on God's power and presence?
2. Are there places where you have stopped asking God for a miracle? Are there spaces where you have stopped believing He can bring external breakthrough?

3. What do we learn about God from Paul's life? What are you learning about God from the season you are currently in?
4. If you prayed for a supernatural breakthrough, what would you ask God to do? What would you ask Him for, believing He would provide?

TODAY'S AFFIRMATION

My Father is a God of miracles. He shakes the very foundations of my life to allow His will to be done. He doesn't just care about my heart; He cares about my circumstances, and He is capable of transforming both. Today, I want to courageously ask Him for a breakthrough because He says nothing is impossible with Him. Even as I feel doubt and fear, I want to hope, because God is working for my good and His glory. By faith, my belief is rising, and I will look for miracles in my life. I want my Father to shake the walls and break the chains, to let His supernatural provision be evident and easy to see. I want to receive His breakthrough with open hands and a grateful heart. I will praise Him when He brings breakthroughs I could never accomplish on my own.

DAY 29

Face Your Fears

The Lord is my shepherd, I lack nothing.
He makes me lie down in green pastures,
he leads me beside quiet waters,
he refreshes my soul.
He guides me along the right paths
for his name's sake.
Even though I walk
through the [valley of the shadow of death]
I will fear no evil,
for you are with me;
your rod and your staff,
they comfort me.

You prepare a table before me
in the presence of my enemies.
You anoint my head with oil;
my cup overflows.
Surely your goodness and love will follow me
all the days of my life,
and I will dwell in the house of the Lord
forever.

Psalm 23

Psalm 23 has been treated unfairly.

It's as though we have taken a terrifying movie and made a cartoon out of it. We've added some throw pillows and plastered sweet pictures of a soft-faced Jesus holding a little lamb beside words written in flowery calligraphy. But let's take it bit by bit to see if it is really as soft and cozy as we have treated it. First, let's think about who penned these words and in what setting.

Theologians have concluded that King David likely wrote Psalm 23 in the later years of his reign, after much pain and heartache, sin and suffering. But he was still clearly influenced by his formative years as a humble shepherd. With some of his story in mind, let's take this beautiful piece of poetry, verse by verse.

"The Lord is my shepherd, I lack nothing."

These words seem simple enough. Knowing David's story, we know that he desired many things, both good and bad. He desired God's glory through his reign, but he was also led by wicked, selfish desires. These observations lead me to conclude that the opening to his prayer is a declaration and reminder that God is the one who must direct and satisfy our longings.

"He makes me lie down in green pastures."

The Hebrew word for "makes me lie down" is *rabats*, and when I study it in the context of the other places it is used in Scripture—it reads a lot like "God lays me out. He puts me on my back. He brings me low." Yes, the setting is beautiful, but this is not an invitation to rest so much as it is a command to do so.

Quiet waters, yes! Soul refreshment, I'll take it!

I want to go down the right path for Your name's sake, God. It's the valley of the shadow of death where I pause. I've looked at the Hebrew, I've studied the concordance, and I've read correlating passages, and there is no sweet way around this one.

Now, in wisdom, we realize that not all paths where God is present with us are peaceful. When we read this verse in correlation with the one before it, we realize it was the Shepherd who actually led us to this terrifying place. The "right path" was not necessarily one that was moving us away from doom, gloom, pain, and potential fear.

That's not something many of us would sign up for.

And then there is the shepherd's rod, conjuring up images of a short, club-like tool used to fight off predators, and a staff with a hook on the end, used to yank a wandering lamb back to safety. As much as I love Jesus, I don't really want to watch helplessly as He clobbers what threatens me, and I sure don't want to be brought back forcefully with a hook into the fold.

What's next down this path?

"You prepare a table before me in the presence of my enemies."

Ah, a fancy dinner with my enemies, the people and forces that want to take me out, witness my demise, and never have my best interests at heart. Oh joy! Lest you think I don't love Psalm 23, I will tell you now that I believe it is an essential passage for our spiritual formation and can be deeply instructional for our hearts. I just don't think it's as sweet as we often assume.

I don't know the particular shadows that are creeping around the corners of your life right now. I don't know what has you so spooked that you would run from the nearness and dearness of Jesus's side. But I have a feeling you are probably motivated by self-preservation. I don't think that being scared of the shadows or wary of your enemies makes you weak. It makes you human. And I also believe that God knows that, that He has compassion for His kids, and that's got to be part of the reason He provides us with a beautiful passage like this.

Because when I try to read this passage in context, there is one major encouragement my heart finds: Jesus is better.

God's presence *is* enough to protect us.

Our path, though it might look perilous right now, can be used for our good and His glory.

No enemy can separate us from His love and faithfulness.

His goodness and faithfulness are chasing after us, and they are better at catching us than our enemies are.

We can't be courageous until we are scared.

We can't know full trust until the path looks dark.

We can't stand in victory until we take His hand.

Let's keep walking.

REFLECTION QUESTIONS

1. What valley of the shadow of death are you walking through right now? Is God with you?
2. How have you responded in the past (or the present) when God has brought you low?
3. Where have you experienced God's protection or provision in the past? Did it feel sweet and flowery or scary and shaky? What did you learn from it?
4. Do you believe that God's goodness and love are following you in this season? What is the evidence of that in your life?

TODAY'S AFFIRMATION

My God is a good Shepherd, and I want to live like I lack nothing. When the path looks shadowy and scary, I want to trust His map more than my own. I want His presence to be all the comfort and confidence I need. His rod and His staff are with me, and He is using them for my good and His glory. I affirm that God's goodness and love are coming toward me, following after me, providing for me, and sustaining me. My Father is enough, even in the hard times. God is enough for me in every season.

DAY 30

Make a Plan and Hold It Loosely

Because I was confident of this, I wanted to visit you first so that you might benefit twice. I wanted to visit you on my way to Macedonia and to come back to you from Macedonia, and then to have you send me on my way to Judea. Was I fickle when I intended to do this? Or do I make my plans in a worldly manner so that in the same breath I say both "Yes, yes" and "No, no"?

2 Corinthians 1:15–17

Do you ever wonder what your role would be in the apocalypse? That may be a weird question, but picture yourself there now. It's the end of the world as we know it. The sky is crashing down, either figuratively or literally, and people are gathered together, cowering against the forces of evil. Where are you in this scenario?

I think I would have two roles: I'd be making the coffee and making a plan.

You wouldn't want me holding a weapon or fighting anyone with my hands. You wouldn't ask me to build the bunker or broker deals between warring enemies. I would drop the sword in fear and run away at the first scratch, and the walls would fall down and the tension would increase. But, I could make a decent pot of coffee, and I could make a plan.

If I approached this book the way I would approach the apocalypse, it would read something like this: *Okay! You're in a season of heartbreak, burnout, and brokenness! Let's list all your pain points! Tell me about your rhythms: How's your sleep? Exercise? Eating? What's your desired outcome, and how can we reverse engineer that? If you know what your first step would be, what would it be, and how can I hold your hand as we take it together?*

But . . . I didn't write that book because my years in ministry have taught me that you can't plan someone out of pain. My own life has taught me that even the best strategy won't help me circumvent a soul-crushing season. Life has taught me that we can make a good, wise plan, and it still might not come to fruition.

Second Corinthians is not necessarily a laid-back letter. Paul has some issues to address regarding the church in Corinth. He's been getting some messy reports; he's heard that they are calling his apostleship into question, and now they are growing restless because he hasn't made it back to the city as quickly as he had planned. To be honest, these very human interactions in the epistles make me love the Word of God even more than I already did. They are so relatable!

And these verses convict me because sometimes I love creating a plan more than I love following my Father. Whether you love a plan or hate it, let's hold our proclivities and current predicament up to Him. During heartbreaking seasons, we typically need one of two encouragements, so take whichever one you're most desperate for today:

If you've just been getting by—grieving, feeling, and letting yourself sit in the ache of whatever you're going through—it might be time to make a plan. Pull out a piece of paper and write down where you want to end up. Start crafting steps that will help you get from here to there. There is nothing wrong with using the wisdom God has given you to begin making moves toward breakthrough.

If you have already made a plan, maybe even thirteen plans, and you are distracted by them not coming to fruition exactly as you had hoped, remember that we make plans, but God directs our steps (see Prov. 16:9). God is not fickle with you, and you are not a failure. Breakthrough is often more spiritual than it is strategic.

Your planning need not be at war with God's perfect, holy ways. Your drive to take forward steps and your need to trust Him with those steps should not be pitted against each other.

Peace can look a lot like passivity, and faith can look a lot like striving, and it takes discernment, trial, and error to find the right balance as we move from brokenness to victory.

In all of this, it is important for us to remember that going from losing to winning isn't a linear path. We can feel broken and believe in wholeness at the same time. We can feel discouraged and declare healing in the same breath. We can have the hardest day and still stand in victory.

Make a plan, but hold it loosely. God can be trusted.

REFLECTION QUESTIONS

1. Is your proclivity to sit still and wait on God or rush ahead and make a plan? What are some of the warning signs that you are doing one or the other in your own power instead of His?
2. Reflect on a time when your plans didn't come to fruition. What did you learn about God? What did you learn about yourself?
3. What does releasing control to God look like in your life? What does it need to look like today?
4. Is it encouraging to remember that the path to victory isn't always linear? How can you continually remind yourself of this truth?

TODAY'S AFFIRMATION

Father, thank You for being a better planner than me. I affirm and agree that, even when my plans seem to fail, You have never failed me. I commit again to let You guide my healing because I trust that You are not fickle. I believe that You are working all things together for my good, even when I can't see it. Help me to hold my plans loosely and to follow Your Spirit's leading with wild worship and peace. I declare that my wisdom and faith are not in opposition to one another, but both are tools to help me walk with You. I will stand in victory, wait on You, and move in humility with every step.

Bless the Boundary Lines

> The boundary lines have fallen for me in pleasant places;
> surely I have a delightful inheritance.
>
> Psalm 16:6

Before my eyes opened on my birthday morning, I silently asked God for a word.

My family is the kind of family that asks God for a word. We want a verse for our birthdays, a literal word for the new year, and we want a fresh encouragement or blessing before any missional endeavor. We like hearing from God. We love hearing from God. We are people who like to get a word.

But I didn't yet have one for the coming year. So, before I opened my eyes that morning, I asked God for a word.

Immediately, Psalm 16:6 popped into my head. I knew the verse by heart, and the phrase began rolling through my brain without provocation.

"The boundary lines have fallen for me in pleasant places."

Without opening my eyes or my mouth, I prayed back to the Lord. "Another one, please? I'm not even sure this one is from You. It might have just popped into my head because I like it."

I clambered to find my glasses in the dark, grabbed my robe, and plodded as quietly as possible toward the living room. It was my birthday morning, but sleeping in was not on the agenda. I wanted to hear from God.

I pulled out some birthday notes that my husband had invited my friends to write for me. I wanted to scan through them and hopefully see a theme or a passage that I could cling to for the coming year. Wouldn't you know? Out of the dozen or so cards, three of them had Psalm 16:6 written on them—including the one from my husband! Now I was starting to pay attention.

I pulled out my pen and journal and began writing.

If I blessed the boundary lines I had been given, I might learn and begin to love the limits of my life.

If I blessed the boundary lines I had been given, I might look to receive and enjoy the pleasant places of my season.

If I blessed the boundary lines I had been given, I might embrace and step into the spiritual inheritance I have been given.

All of this sounds spiritual and sweet, right? The hard part is that on the morning of this particular birthday, I was in the thick of the hardest season of my life. I didn't want to bless these boundary lines—I wanted new ones.

In these moments, we can remind ourselves of this: *This season is not happening to me; it is happening for me.*

If I believe in a good and loving Father who uses every ounce of pain and hardship in my life for my good and His glory, then there is not a single instance of heartbreak, burnout, or brokenness that can slip through His hands. He has not grown careless with me, and He is never surprised when I encounter the pain of living in this fallen world.

He saw this coming, and in His love and care, He allowed it. He has walked with me, sustained me, upheld me, empowered me, taught me, grown me, used me, and now He is inviting me to use my own words to bless even *these* boundary lines.

I cannot simply affirm the territories of my life that are beautiful and easy, knowing full well they're gifts from Him, if I do not also affirm that He is with me in the terrible seasons as well.

This season is not happening to me; it is happening *for* me.

And I don't just believe that God cares for me. I don't just believe that healing is mine for the taking. And I don't just believe that victory will one day be mine. I can walk in authority and declare that I have a beautiful inheritance right here and now, even in this pain, in Jesus's name.

You don't have to say it until you're ready. In fact, I suggest you don't. We can't gaslight ourselves into giving God glory. There is no faking it until you make it in the kingdom of God. There are just honest humans with shaky and humble voices, doing their best to trust God with the truth they speak. And if you listen closely, you will hear them say,

> The boundary lines have fallen for me in pleasant
> places;
> surely I have a delightful inheritance.

REFLECTION QUESTIONS

1. What do the boundary lines look like in your life right now? Have you been hesitant to embrace them? Why?

2. Reflect on and remember a past season of pain. How and where did you find purpose in it?
3. Does it bring you comfort or courage to declare, "This season is not happening to me; it is happening for me"? If not, how does it make you feel?
4. What would it look like to bless the boundary lines you have been given in this season? How do you think it might change your experience of this time?

TODAY'S AFFIRMATION

My Father, I bless You for the boundaries You have established for me. I may not welcome them or understand them, but I trust You have a good and kind plan for me. Help me to bless these boundaries, believing that within them lies my inheritance, which is a good and perfect gift from You. Help me to walk in the kingdom authority of peace, purpose, and freedom that Jesus purchased for me on the cross. I want to believe that my inheritance is not just in future healing or the absence of hardship but that it is here, right now. In Jesus's name, I affirm that the boundary lines have indeed fallen for me in pleasant places. Amen.

DAY 32

Tell the Truth and Shame the Devil

> They triumphed over him
> by the blood of the Lamb
> and by the word of their testimony;
> they did not love their lives so much
> as to shrink from death.
>
> Revelation 12:11

I have teen drivers, so I know a thing or two about sudden turns.

There's nothing more jarring than feeling smooshed up against the passenger window as the driver to your left pulls the wheel with no warning and your body takes the brunt of the surprise shift. So this is me saying, "Quick turn coming up!" Enjoy the ride; it's going to take us somewhere fun.

We're taking a quick turn from Paul and the Psalms to visit John on the island of Patmos, inside the words of the book of Revelation.

I don't approach Revelation lightly or under any pretense that it is a book people easily relate to or comprehend.

Like so much of the New Testament, it's a letter written to a specific people group that also has wild and beautiful insight and implications for the modern church.

There are theologians who believe Revelation 12 depicts a battle that will happen and theologians who believe that battle has already occurred. But either way, the end result is clear: The enemy loses; the kingdom of God wins. It's just these seven little words that have stuck in my head for the last few years: "and by the word of their testimony . . ."

The accuser, the enemy, the thief who came to kill, steal, and destroy is defeated. He is "hurled down," as John the beloved describes. And we are never left wondering who the hero is in this scenario because it is so clearly our conquering King, our Friend and Savior, Jesus Christ.

But "they" who get to play a part in that triumph are the brothers and sisters, the believers. The addition they bring to the fight isn't might or skillful fighting but the word of their testimony.

I don't know what season of heaviness or hardship you find yourself in today. But I do know who is to blame for brokenness in this world—it's the enemy.

And you and I could sit in the midst of the carnage and suffering around us, striving and wondering how in the world we'll fix it, how we'll push the enemy back, and how we'll take back the ground, land, and time that he has tried to steal from us.

But in the end, it's Jesus who brings breakthrough, wins the war, accomplishes healing, and gets the glory.

Our part, seemingly, is to open our mouths and tell about what He has done.

So, this is your invitation to start now. In a startlingly simple way, I want to invite you to tell the truth and shame the devil.

Get loud about what God has done for you. Write out a list of the ways He has sustained you. Testify to the healing you've already seen. Declare His glory and goodness to anyone who will listen. Do not be shy about sharing the word of your testimony, not only once the breakthrough has arrived but right now—get loud and proclaim His faithfulness in the midst of your heartbreak or burnout.

This is how we take back what was stolen.

This is how we defeat the enemy.

This is how we walk in authority.

This is how we see breakthrough.

We tell the truth about what God has done for us and shame the spineless enemy who wants us to believe that He has been anything other than good.

Amen?

REFLECTION QUESTIONS

1. Where have you specifically seen God's faithfulness in the past? Where has He brought breakthrough in previous seasons of heartbreak, burnout, or brokenness?
2. What doubts or fears have kept you from sharing your testimony in the past?
3. How can you actively "get loud" about what God has done for you, both in personal conversations and within your community?
4. What are you waiting on to walk in the authority Christ has given you? What do you feel is missing for you to claim the strength you have access to in Jesus's name?

TODAY'S AFFIRMATION

Father, today and all days, I stand in awe of Your unwavering faithfulness. Today and all days, I choose to boldly declare the testimony of Your goodness in my life. I refuse to let fear silence me, knowing that my words have brought and will bring defeat to the enemy and glory to Your name. You have been my Sustainer, my Healer, my Victory. As I speak of past and present victories You have brought, I walk in the authority You have given me, reclaiming all that the enemy has tried to steal. Let my voice be a light in the dark, a reminder to all who hear, that You are good, God, and never fail. In Jesus's mighty name, amen.

DAY 33

Let's Get Dressed

> Finally, be strong in the Lord and in his mighty power. Put on the full armor of God, so that you can take your stand against the devil's schemes.
>
> Ephesians 6:10–11

In my family, the ladies like to coordinate outfits. I don't mean we like to match colors or patterns when we show up at the same place, but we do like to make sure we're all within the same outfit *vibe*, if you will.

There's nothing worse than dressing up and arriving to find your sisters in cute sweat suits. Except for, maybe, misunderstanding the moment as casual when everyone else is dressed to the nines. Knowing what to wear and when helps us feel prepared. It helps us feel present. It helps us know what is expected of us. And God's Word knows this about us.

If reading and comprehending God's Word were as simple as smooshing verses together, Revelation 12 mixed with Ephesians 6 would give us such a strong understanding of what it looks like to experience breakthrough.

I've prayed and labored about the best way to send us out in our authority in Christ Jesus. I've wrestled with the Lord over what I sense Him wanting me to say versus what I'd really like to say to seal this season of breakthrough we have walked through together.

In His kindness and goodness, I sense that He has let me experience this truth in multiple areas of my life so that I could say it to you with authority: Our circumstances may not have changed. The brokenness, fatigue, heartache, and pain that led us to these forty days together may not have subsided, and we may not see any release or shift in our situation. But we have changed. He has grown us. We have been strengthened. We have experienced breakthrough as His light and healing have hit our hearts, as our minds have changed, our fortitude has been strengthened, and our spiritual muscles have developed for His glory and our good.

But that's still not the end of the story.

Because if we're both incredibly honest, we know what's next.

There will be more heartache, burnout, and brokenness in the future.

So, we get dressed. And we stand.

What's wild about the armor of God isn't just that it's multiple pieces of protection gear with one offensive weapon thrown in. What's wild about the armor of God isn't just that we're instructed to put on all these things just so we can stay still. What's maybe wilder to me (than anything else) about the armor of God is that it's one way God signifies to us (and the enemy) just who we belong to. Because what is more signifying of the side you're on than your uniform?

The armor protects us from future attacks. The armor reminds the enemy that our souls are spoken for. And the armor enables us to stand firm.

I wish we could spend the last days of this devotional, our time together, just celebrating our breakthroughs so far and basking in the glory of a life that is figured out and tidied up. I wish we could tie a bow on our stories and narrate God's glory throughout the ups and downs that have already happened. I wish we could say, "We've made it through this fight, and that's all there is."

But the truth is, you and I will encounter pain again and again this side of heaven. The truth is, we were strengthened for this battle, and we'll use what we learned during future attacks on our wholeness. The truth is, any healing, victory, or authority we've been handed in this season of breakthrough will be needed for the brokenness ahead.

But we don't have to be scared.

Our God will do the heavy lifting.

But we do have to be prepared.

So let's get dressed, in Jesus's name.

REFLECTION QUESTIONS

1. How does it feel to know, or remember, that there will be future battles where you'll need future breakthroughs? Conversely, how does it feel to know that all you have to do is stand?
2. In what ways do you feel strengthened by God from this past season?
3. Where do you currently feel the most vulnerable and in need of the armor of God?
4. How can you remind yourself that the armor of God signifies your belonging to Him, especially when faced with fear or uncertainty?

TODAY'S AFFIRMATION

Father, thank You for the armor You have provided, the divine protection that guards my heart, mind, and soul. I want to notice and declare today how far You have brought me, how safe You have kept me, even as I've walked through wild pain and disappointment. Today, I choose to stand firm, not in my own strength but in the power of Your might. I want to put on the full armor of God because I need You and Your protection and because I want to remind myself and the enemy of my soul of this truth: I am Yours, and no weapon formed against me will prosper. I know future battles will come, but I trust that You will do the heavy lifting. In every future fight, I will stand my ground, knowing that You have equipped me for victory. In Jesus's name, Amen.

DAY 34

Don't Get Distracted

> For our struggle is not against flesh and blood, but against the rulers, against the authorities, against the powers of this dark world and against the spiritual forces of evil in the heavenly realms.
>
> Ephesians 6:12

I wanted to blame the church volunteer.

The one who was unkind to my husband (his pastor), writing him dismissive emails and making assumptions about his decisions and intentions.

It was a tense time, a heavy season, and I was watching Nick, in real time, labor over how to lead him because he genuinely wanted to see this guy win. Nick would spend hours praying over a particular email, rewriting it, and trying to get his words just so. And then the volunteer would reply quickly, dismissing Nick's attempts to bring peace.

I wanted to blame him when Nick started having panic attacks. But in truth, it wasn't his fault. Just like I wanted to blame the doctor who performed my stepdad's surgery. I saw him at the grocery store a few weeks after the funeral, and my whole body went cold. I just happened to be wearing the same sweatshirt in the store that I had worn the day of the surgery, and it was all too eerie. I wondered if he recognized me, and I got even more flushed when I realized he probably didn't; he had lots of patients, and they all had a story. I wanted to blame him, but I knew in my gut it wasn't his fault. He had tried his best, and we live in a fallen world.

I wanted to blame every person who asked me for a favor when my family was struggling. Didn't they know I was trying to keep my head above water? But no, they didn't. Because our pain was kept private on purpose, to protect our kids and let their story be their story.

When heartbreak, burnout, and brokenness abound, you and I can probably spot multiple people to blame, including ourselves.

I wanted to blame myself the most.

I would sit on our sofa on the darkest days and ask my husband, "Do you think I broke all this? If I had prayed more, worked less, would things be different? Am I the problem?"

I wanted to blame myself, just like I wanted to blame everyone else, but even that proved fruitless in the end.

A woman who walks with true kingdom authority and freedom knows exactly where the blame should go. And walking in that authority means we have to stay laser-focused on the real enemy by not getting distracted by flesh and blood and blaming people who are just as broken as we are.

You and I must keep the enemy the enemy.

So, to be explicitly clear, the enemy of our souls is the only enemy worth fighting.

Allowing the enemy to be the enemy does not mean I ignore my current pain. It does not mean I never tell people when they have hurt me or wisely set boundaries on future pain they may inflict. Remembering that the enemy is the enemy does help me, however, humbly remember that I could easily be the enemy in someone else's story. Ultimately, my active and ongoing anger is directed at the enemy of our souls because I believe he is the one who is trying to steal, kill, and destroy my perception of abundance.

Our fight isn't with flesh and blood. Our fight isn't even with our own flesh, or our own fallenness.

Let's not get distracted by placing blame on souls that were never meant to carry something this heavy. Let's not get distracted by fighting with other people when the principalities are the ones we should be focusing on. Let's own the authority that is ours in Christ Jesus and aim our fight in the right direction. Let's fight for new life where Satan has tried to kill. Let's get mad at the right enemy for what he has tried to steal. Let's get riled up for the precious abundance he has tried to destroy.

If by grace through faith, we walk with Jesus, we walk with the authority to demolish every stronghold and pretension that sets itself up against the knowledge of God. That means this is a fight we can win.

Stand firm and remember that the enemy is the enemy.

REFLECTION QUESTIONS

1. Who are you most likely to blame during hardship? And how can you release them, or yourself, from that anger and frustration?

2. How can you remind yourself to stay focused on fighting the real enemy—Satan and his schemes—when dealing with challenging people or situations?
3. What practices can you implement to protect yourself from taking on unnecessary blame or shame?
4. Where do you need to reclaim authority over the enemy's attempts to steal, kill, and destroy?

TODAY'S AFFIRMATION

I am a much-loved child of God, and my battle is not against flesh and blood but rather against the spiritual forces of darkness that seek to steal my breakthrough. I reject the invitation to distraction that would be found in a cycle of blame or shame. There is therefore no condemnation for those who are in Christ Jesus, including me. In the name of Jesus, I take authority by staying alert to the schemes of my enemy, and I will stand firm in the truth of Your Word. The principalities of hell have no power over me, and I will not be deceived into fighting battles that aren't mine to fight. I embrace the abundant life You have given me, trusting that You have already won the victory.

DAY 35

Bring Your Belt

Stand firm then, with the belt of truth buckled around your waist.

Ephesians 6:14

I'm going to tell you the most embarrassing story of my life.

When people ask, usually in groups or at a party, "What's the most embarrassing thing that's ever happened to you?" I do not speak up. This is not a story you tell at a party. Nevertheless, here I am, sharing it in a book.

In our early days of ministry, when my husband was a new pastor and I was just a doe-eyed pastor's wife, he was pulled aside for a carefrontation. If you're not familiar, a carefrontation is a meeting that is held with the explicit purpose of telling you what you've done wrong.

Unfortunately for me, this meeting was not about something Nick had done or not done. It was just about me. I want to believe the intention was more care than confrontation—but it doesn't make the memory any more enjoyable.

Can we just pause to acknowledge how awkward and wrong it is to approach someone's spouse when you really want to correct them? Nothing is more uncomfortable than having to sit through a meeting where you want to defend your husband or wife. Except maybe having to go home and tell your spouse everything you just heard.

Nick came to me sheepishly after the meeting. I knew immediately from the look on his face that I was the problem.

"What have I done now?" I asked begrudgingly. Spoiler alert: This was not a community we stayed in long, as my very presence seemed to agitate people.

"Well . . . it's been suggested that you need . . ."

I asked him to spit it out.

"A belt."

My face immediately turned fifteen shades of red, then purple, then white, and then back to red again. I was mortified.

I had recently had our fourth baby and knew my clothes weren't fitting well. My prepregnancy pants were too tight, and I could barely keep the maternity jeans up. Dear friends, I didn't even own a belt. These were lean years. Your girl was on a budget. But apparently, a few of the other women had commented to their husbands and church leaders that my pants didn't seem to fit well. And apparently, I was exposing more of myself than I intended as I carried my new baby in and out of their car seat and chased my toddlers around the church parking lot in a sleepless, newborn haze.

Recalling this story, I don't know how I ever showed back up to church again. I can't remember if I was more mad or embarrassed, but in recounting it now, I can feel deep and persistent shame rise up in me all over again.

One thing I learned from this experience: A belt keeps you from exposing more than you want to.

How exposed have we already felt, friends, from the heartbreak, burnout, and brokenness in our lives? How tenderly have we let the air hit our most vulnerable places: our weaknesses, our desire for healing, our identities, and our hopes? How long have we walked around, our souls like one large, exposed nerve, always on the edge of crying, cracking, or causing a stir?

We have lived exposed just by living. We need not live more exposed by allowing the enemy of our souls to lead us in lies.

We need not be caught unprotected from his schemes, his lies, or his extensive strategy to derail us from a life poured out for God's glory.

I had every excuse in that season to forgo a belt.

Who wants to wear a belt when you're nursing a baby?

You have every excuse to take a break from pursuing the truth of God with reckless abandon. Maybe there is too much heartache in your midst to sit and study the Word, or you're too tired and fatigued to make it to church, or the brokenness that blows all around you is all the reason you need to avoid wise counsel.

But the truth is, it's too tender a time to relinquish your authority to the one who cannot be trusted.

You have access to the belt of truth.

Put it on, stand firm, and see healing begin to break through in your life.

REFLECTION QUESTIONS

1. In what areas of your life do you feel the most exposed or vulnerable, and how can you protect yourself by putting on truth?
2. Are there any lies from the enemy that you have allowed to shape the way you see yourself or your current season?

3. What has kept you from surrounding yourself with truth on a daily basis?
4. Where can you practice rhythms of truth in your life right now? Daily Bible reading? Listening to sermons? Asking for wise counsel?

TODAY'S AFFIRMATION

I refuse to be left vulnerable and exposed to the enemy of my soul. Especially when I have access to the armor of God and eternal truth at my fingertips. I reject the pretense that sets itself up against the knowledge of God, and I reject any scheme that has been created to expose or shame me. In my moments of weakness, in moments of strength, I will surround myself with the promises of God because He is my Mighty Fortress. I will pursue His truth with boldness, even in the midst of brokenness and fatigue. I trust the Lord, and I know that in His truth I am secure.

DAY 36

Just Put On the Vest

Stand firm then, . . . with the breastplate of righteousness in place.

Ephesians 6:14

I don't watch scary movies.

I don't play around with ghosts.

You will never catch me watching a movie or television show where someone is demon-possessed because I don't mess with the devil like that. I'm not judging you if you watch them. I don't think you're opening spiritual portals or ruining your family. I am just way too terrified to be messing with satanic stuff in my entertainment.

What I do enjoy, however, is a good action movie. Would I like to watch a police chase through heavily crowded streets? Yes, please! An ongoing thriller where two spies might be outed for months on end? Sign me up! Throw in some counterintelligence, covert ops, a soundtrack that brings your heart to the edge of panic, and I'm a happy camper. Top it off with buttered popcorn, and you've got a beautiful night.

But do you know what my absolute favorite thing is to happen in an action movie? When it turns out the hero, who you just watched crumple to the ground, presumably dead, with his partner turned secret girlfriend screaming in the background, was actually wearing a *bulletproof vest the entire time*.

For a few hours after watching a scene like this, I find myself thinking, *Would it be such a bad idea to wear a bulletproof vest all the time? Shouldn't we all have one, just in case?* Then I realize that I can barely remember to carry an extra jacket around with me.

But imagine having access to protection like this *spiritually*.

Imagine having a layer that keeps you from inevitable and egregious wounding in the battles that are to come. Imagine feeling less scared, more courageous, and more settled in your soul because you don't have to spend your energy working to protect or prove anything about your identity or worth.

This is the beauty of the breastplate of righteousness.

When we move through seasons of heartbreak, burnout, or brokenness, there is often more than our grief, fatigue, and pain at play. The shame we feel is often more palpable than what's actually plaguing us. The condemnation and accusations that threaten to wound our sense of security, our identity, and our understanding of our worth are the body blows that often leave us unwilling or unable to even stand back up in the midst of our trials.

We wonder what we could have done differently.

We wonder if we're to blame.

We wonder if it would be so hard if we were stronger.

We wonder if we are the problem and if everyone else is living an easier life because they are better, more blessed, or just more valuable to our Father.

But what does the breastplate of righteousness mean for us? What has been given to us?

> It is because of him that you are in Christ Jesus, who has become for us wisdom from God—that is, our righteousness, holiness and redemption. (1 Cor. 1:30)

> For by grace you have been saved through faith. And this is not your own doing; it is the gift of God, not a result of works, so that no one may boast. (Eph. 2:8–9 ESV)

> Indeed, I count everything as loss because of the surpassing worth of knowing Christ Jesus my Lord. For his sake I have suffered the loss of all things and count them as rubbish, in order that I may gain Christ and be found in him, not having a righteousness of my own that comes from the law, but that which comes through faith in Christ, the righteousness from God that depends on faith. (Phil. 3:8–9 ESV)

We don't earn, sustain, keep, or secure our own righteousness. Therefore, we cannot be found out. We cannot be condemned. We didn't cause any of the good in our life; it was all a gift from God, and we cannot bear the weight of the bad as if it is all ours to ward off.

When the enemy of our souls comes for us in this season of hardship or the next, we can stand secure and firm, knowing that Jesus's righteousness has spoken for our souls.

This is more powerful than any bulletproof vest. We don't have to remember to bring it with us, and it holds secure in the face of any accusation, including the ones coming from our own mind. What's more, we cannot "pay" God for our breakthrough with good behavior. His comfort in hardship is a mercy, and His hand moving in our circumstances is a miracle. The best we can hope for is to posture our hearts to allow healing to happen internally first and foremost.

Whatever happens next, what is *always* true is our security in Jesus, even if and when more pain comes our way. We have access to a supernatural safeguard who speaks over our lives and promises to keep our hearts soft, the way they function best.

REFLECTION QUESTIONS

1. Where do you currently feel shame or condemnation?
2. How have you tried to earn your righteousness in the past? How might you still be trying to pay for your breakthrough with good behavior?
3. What would you do if you felt fully safe and secure in Jesus's name?
4. How do you want to keep your heart soft, protected by His righteousness, for future battles?

TODAY'S AFFIRMATION

I agree and thank God that I am covered by the righteousness of Christ. I do not have to earn, protect, or prove myself worthy of supernatural security.

Lord, Your gift of righteousness keeps me safe amid every battle, accusation, and hardship. I declare that I am free from condemnation and shame, because You speak for my soul. I stand firm in the knowledge that I am Yours, and nothing can separate me from Your love. As I move forward, I will wear the breastplate of righteousness with confidence, knowing that You have equipped me for every trial.

DAY 37

Are You Ready Yet?

> Stand firm then, . . . with your feet fitted with the readiness that comes from the gospel of peace.
>
> Ephesians 6:14–15

I blame the fact that I'm a linear thinker and also a middle child.

One of my biggest weaknesses is that I need a clear delineation at all times, almost an explicit map drawn, to tell me who we are focusing on at the moment: you or me.

I don't do well with the gray or the in-between when it comes to knowing who the focus is on.

Maybe it's also because I'm a woman who spent her formative years being trained in ministry. What I'm trying to say is that I don't see in purple. Here's what I mean:

A few months ago, my husband and I were heading into a workout class together when I got some good news. It was the stuff of miracles and something I had been praying about for years. Nick dropped everything to celebrate with me, making the biggest fuss by cheering for me and thanking God with me.

He even encouraged me to come into the workout class late so I could call my mom and sisters and said he would set up all the equipment I needed. He wanted me to savor this good news, and he was really, really happy for me.

When I made my way into the workout, a silly smile still plastered on my face, he hugged me again and then mentioned how this was actually potentially good news for him too. I hadn't thought about it, but he was right! This was a blessing in my life that was also going to benefit the people around me. And as we started moving through the class, I couldn't stop thinking about it.

My husband is the least self-serving person you will ever meet. He would bend over backward for me to experience blessing. But here he was, able to see both the upside for me and the upside for him. Miraculous? Outstanding? Novel? Not so much, unless you're a middle child who is also a serious linear thinker and who was raised in ministry and taught that only one person can give and receive at a time.

I told him after the class that I wanted to get better at seeing in purple. I often think, *This would be good for me!* or *This would be good for Nick!* I see in red or blue. But I rarely see in purple.

This is easy to talk about when we're discussing blessing, but it becomes more difficult when talking about pain.

When I am hurting, when I am tired, or when I am at the end of my rope, there is a valve that squeezes shut somewhere in my heart. When this happens, I can't think about other people. I have to take care of myself. In my flesh, I think, *I can't love people and experience wild heartache at the same time. I can't worship and also be worried about what's going to happen to me. I can't be generous and also protect what little I have in this hardship.* I can't see purple while I am experiencing pain.

Only, there is a word in Ephesians 6 about feet fitted with a readiness that can only come from the gospel of peace.

Theologians have multiple perspectives regarding the meaning of this passage. Because the Greek words translate almost literally to "boots of peace," interpreters are often split on whether this means the one who wears the armor is given "firmness of feet" or a "readiness to share the Good News." But either way, the juxtaposition of "peace" in the midst of a passage on warfare should bring us to pause.

Here's what I know: In the midst of pain, knowing that I am a child of God and can receive His care feels a lot like worship. It feels like embracing my identity in the purest sense.

When I'm going through heartbreak or burnout, taking steps toward healing feels like something I get to do rather than just living wounded for the rest of my days.

In hardship, standing up and seeing the spiritual victory that is mine for the taking feels wild and beautiful, and I am so grateful for that grace.

But then to look down at my feet and see that they are ready to bring peace to others? That feels like wild, beautiful, purple authority.

When I can start to look around and see not only how the blessings in my life have blessed others but also how the hardships in my life have affected those who love me? That feels like a sobering and beautiful authority. And to feel ready to bring peace, not just to receive it? That feels like a breakthrough.

REFLECTION QUESTIONS

1. How do you find yourself responding in painful seasons? Do you focus on taking care of yourself or sacrifice your needs to care for others?
2. How has God brought peace into your life, even amid this pain, burnout, or hardship?
3. What would it look like for you to see both blessing and hardship in "purple," where your experiences of both benefit not just you but those around you?
4. Are you ready to bring peace in this season? There is no wrong answer.

TODAY'S AFFIRMATION

Lord, I thank You for the readiness that comes from the gospel of peace. Even in the midst of pain, You have equipped me to stand firm and bring Your peace into the lives of others. I declare that I will no longer see my trials and blessings in isolation but will trust You to work in the "purple" places, blending my life with the lives of those around me in a way that brings healing and hope. You have given me both security and purpose, and I am grateful for the authority to share Your peace, even when I'm walking through difficult seasons. In Jesus's name, amen.

Maybe Just Pretend It's Fireworks

In addition to all this, take up the shield of faith, with which you can extinguish all the flaming arrows of the evil one.

Ephesians 6:16

Have you ever heard that anxiety and excitement present the same way in your body?

While excitement is connected to joy, anxiety is often connected to fear, but our bodies can't really differentiate which is which. Our pulse quickens, our breathing changes, and we might sweat or have swirly feelings in our stomach. But which is about to happen, something great or something terrible?

You can't gaslight yourself into believing that anxiety is excitement, but goodness gracious, it would be helpful if you could.

In the same way, I wish we could pretend that the flaming arrows from the enemy of our souls were just fireworks whizzing around us. I wish we could pretend we are just playing laser tag when it really feels like we are in a fight for our lives. It would be so helpful if we could just shift our perspective and suddenly not feel terrified about what is happening to us, near us, or inside of us as we fight heartbreak, burnout, and brokenness.

You can't just pretend that the pain whizzing past you is beautiful, but you can pick up the shield of faith.

What piece of our armor has been given for protection in this portion of Scripture?

The Greek here is pretty straightforward as faith, *pistis*, which is the root word, and the same one we see used in much of the New Testament to denote belief in Jesus. I love how *Strong's Concordance* unpacks this spiritual power as a "collective divine persuasion," the ability we receive as believers in Jesus to be sure of what we hope for and certain of what we cannot see.[1] To put it even more explicitly, this gift we're given by God has the supernatural capacity to extinguish every flame (lie, untruth, or fear) that comes to destroy us and our trust in His goodness and grace.

Do you want to know something wild about a shield?

It only works if you're holding it in front of you, facing the enemy.

The shield is no longer effective if you turn and run. The shield cannot protect you if you drop it and abandon the fight. The shield works best when you hold it, standing still and resolute, with eyes open, looking forward, no matter how tempting it would be to drop everything and run.

As I think about coming to the end of these forty days, I continue to pray for breakthrough. For you and for me. I genuinely hope that we have allowed God to meet us in our pain and

---

1. *Strong's Expanded Exhaustive Concordance of the Bible* (Thomas Nelson, 2009), under "pistis."

fatigue and that we have arrived at a place where we can receive His compassion and companionship, even on the darkest days of our lives. I pray that we've started to heal from whatever harmed us and that fresh wounds have turned into scabs and maybe even into scars, however tender they might remain. I hope that, like me, you have started to believe in victory, even if it doesn't look the way you initially pictured it. May God continually replace our desire for earthly winning with a desire for kingdom come.

But I know that, for many of us, walking forward in authority will include encountering more fiery arrows in our future. And that's a tough pill to swallow.

You can't just pretend they are fireworks.

We live in a fallen world, opposite an enemy who wants nothing more than for us to run like cowards from every future fight. The enemy wants us weaker than when we arrived, more frightened and less resolute. He wants us so triggered by the sound of battle that we can't imagine making it through this season without constantly wondering when the next shoe might drop.

But we know better.

We know we can trust in the One who has brought us this far. We know we can trust in the enemy's eventual demise. We know we can hold up our faith, which has only been made stronger in this particular fight, for whatever is ahead.

You can't pretend deadly arrows are fireworks, but we know who wins this fight. And that makes all the difference.

REFLECTION QUESTIONS

1. How can you remind yourself to pick up your faith when you're tempted to run scared?
2. What are the "arrows" that are currently coming at you? What truths about God can bolster your faith and help you to stand steadfast in this battle?
3. How does knowing that ultimate victory is in Christ change your perspective of the battles you face? How can you continually remind yourself of this truth?
4. Can you write an affirmation for yourself for future fights? Write a short statement or prayer you can recite in the coming season, using what you've learned in this one.

TODAY'S AFFIRMATION

Father, I bless You for this shield of faith You have given me, and I agree that it extinguishes every flaming arrow the enemy throws my way. I declare that I will stand firm, facing forward with my faith held high, trusting in Your power and protection. My eyes are on You; my hopes are up. When lies, fears, and doubts form against me, I will not retreat or run but rather remain resolute. You are my victory. I affirm that, in every battle, You are strengthening my faith, and no weapon formed against me will prosper. In Jesus's name, amen.

What's Saving Your Life Right Now?

Take the helmet of salvation and the sword of the Spirit, which is the word of God. And pray in the Spirit on all occasions with all kinds of prayers and requests. With this in mind, be alert and always keep on praying for all the Lord's people.

Ephesians 6:17–18

The phrase made its way around the block recently.

Podcasters, bloggers, and social media personalities have been posing the question: *What's saving your life right now?*

The answer is always tongue in cheek but earnest.

Maybe it's a book. (As an author, I'm grateful.)

A skin-care product. (As a woman over forty, I can appreciate this.)

A new rhythm for checking in with your sister. (Sometimes the voice memos on your phone stop working.)

An inspiring movie. (I fall asleep during most movies, but maybe you're different.)

If I could go back to the first day of our journey together, I wonder what you might have believed then would save your life in the forty days to come.

These are the words I wrote on Day 1:

The moments when your knees hit the floor.

When your stomach drops.

When the doctor says the thing, and all of a sudden, you can't breathe.

When the door closes behind the person you never thought would leave.

Maybe, if we are honest, we hoped that if we read about a forty-day journey to breakthrough, we would see a reversal in our pain, a cosmic rewind.

Maybe the knees that had hit the floor would now be jumping for joy at good news.

Maybe the grief- and trauma-induced nausea would have turned to physical peace.

Maybe that person would walk back through our door.

Maybe the sinking feeling of *How did we get here?* would be replaced with an awe-inspired *Look at what God has done.*

And for many of us, the circumstances that led us to start this journey have probably shifted for the better. Some have seen prayers answered and miracles crop up in our midst, and the answer to what comes next has been healing and increased hope.

But maybe, for the rest of us, nothing has changed externally. Our hearts have shifted, but our best-case-scenario prayers have not come to fruition.

What's saving *our* life lately?

This is the moment where the full measure of our faith is tested. I don't believe that our righteousness is up for debate because that is found in Jesus alone. I don't believe we will be put on trial for lack of trust because God knows and makes space for our humanity and accommodates our moments of weakness. Many of us are seeing the gap between what we say we believe (our formal belief) and how we live (our functional belief). We are coming to grips with which of these we truly worship: a God we can't always understand or things going exactly the way we want.

I say this with no shame, no blame, and no pride: Right now many of us are coming to terms with the fact that while our formal belief is that Christ is enough, our functional belief says something different.

That one prayer may still be unanswered.

That person may still be gone.

The diagnosis may not have been reversed.

That bill may still be past due.

The crisis may still be unfolding. In fact, it might have gotten worse.

Your fatigue may still be paralyzing.

Or maybe the light has started to break through.

That prayer may have been answered more than you could have asked or imagined.

The person you were missing may be back in your life, relationship restored.

The tests may have come back and in your favor.

A miraculous check, job, or source of provision may have been provided.

Healing may be swirling all around you.

The light may be back in your eyes.

You might feel like you are seeing in color again.

Either way, this season has shifted us.

We may not know what comes next, but we know what is true right now: Our salvation is still firmly found in Christ alone. And that's enough.

REFLECTION QUESTIONS

1. What have you been hoping would "save your life" in this season?
2. How has your understanding of salvation shifted or grown through this season of suffering?
3. How do you maintain your faith when prayers go unanswered? How do you maintain your dependence on God when things go your way?
4. In what ways has God's salvation already rescued you from certain situations, mindsets, or fears during these past forty days?

TODAY'S AFFIRMATION

Father, my salvation is found in You alone. I break ties with anything else I have trusted to "save my life." No matter what circumstances surround me, whether prayers are answered the way I hoped or not, You are enough. I trust in Your goodness and Your timing, knowing that my life is held secure in Your hands. Even when I don't understand the way forward, I choose to stand firm, with the helmet of salvation protecting my mind and the sword of Your Spirit empowering me to press on. You are my refuge, my strength, and my Savior. You are always what comes next, and You are enough.

Here's the Plan

> Now to him who is able to do immeasurably more than all we ask or imagine, according to his power that is at work within us, to him be glory in the church and in Christ Jesus throughout all generations, for ever and ever! Amen.
>
> Ephesians 3:20–21

My superpower and my greatest weakness are all wrapped up in the same personality trait: I love a good plan.

If I have a plan, a path, a linear way forward, I can bear almost anything.

On the contrary, even beautiful moments are overwhelming for me in the worst way if they arrive unplanned.

And so, this question, "What comes next?" is one that reverberates throughout every lonely and languished corner of my life. I have asked this question with you because it is the one that is most often on my tongue.

I asked the doctor, "What comes next?" as I wiped away tears in the waiting room at the hospital.

The words escaped my mouth as I cried into my husband's chest when one of our kids was going through a crisis.

"What will come next?" I sighed as I sat with a friend, processing the trials of this past year.

I wrote the words in my journal, longingly, during prayer time with the Lord.

I have said so many times in this book, "I don't know what this season holds for you." And it's true. I don't know the layers of heartbreak, the trials of burnout, or the different flavors of brokenness that have permeated your life and soul as you have read through this book.

And since I don't know God's particular plan for me and my own circumstances, I certainly can't begin to guess what kind of beauty He is planning to bring from the ashes in your life or how He will do it. I don't know what style or type of redemption He has in mind.

I don't know what comes next. But I do know that you and I are not powerless. We don't have to be passive in this pain. We have a choice.

Will we worship while we wait for healing?

Will we trust God when it doesn't make sense?

Will we pray, pounding heaven day after day, begging God to move?

Will we speak life when others are speaking death?

Will we celebrate and usher in joy even in the midst of pain?

Will we serve and use our gifts even though we are hurting?

Will we forgive?

Will we get our hopes up?

Will we continue letting God meet us with compassion?

Will we get ready to fight?

Will we stand firm when the arrows fly past?

Will we seek to stay faithful?

Will we keep reminding ourselves and others that God is faithful?

Will we grab hold of the breakthrough that is ours for the taking?

Don't believe the lie that what comes next has nothing to do with you.

You and I are not hapless victims of this season; we are children of God who have access to the power that raised Jesus Christ from the dead. We are free from condemnation, have been given a spirit of love and a sound mind, and released from the chains of fear and death.

We may not know His exact plan, but we do know what comes next: God's power made perfect in our weakness so that He might be glorified and we might be reconciled to Him and one another.

REFLECTION QUESTIONS

1. What has God done in your life and heart over the last forty days?
2. What has God done in the people around you over the last forty days?
3. What questions do you still have about what comes next?
4. What do you know to be true about what comes next?

TODAY'S AFFIRMATION

Write your own prayer of affirmation to end this season. God is mighty in you.

JESS CONNOLLY

is the author of several books, including *Tired of Being Tired.* She and her husband, Nick, planted Bright City Church in Charleston, South Carolina, where they live with their four children. As the lead coach and founder of Go + Tell Gals and the host of *The Jess Connolly Podcast,* Jess wants to leave her generation more in awe of God than she found it. She's passionate about her family, women, God's Word, and the local church.

CONNECT WITH JESS

JessConnolly.com